WITHDRAWN

WALKING
VENICE

WALKING
VENICE

THE BEST OF THE CITY

Joe Yogerst and Gillian Price

NATIONAL GEOGRAPHIC

Washington, D.C.

WALKING
VENICE

CONTENTS

PART 1

PAGE 12
WHIRLWIND TOURS

PART 2

PAGE 50
VENICE'S NEIGHBORHOODS

PART 3

PAGE 170
TRAVEL ESSENTIALS

Previous pages: Piazzetta San Marco; left: dressed for Carnevale; right: the Ponte di Rialto; above right: clockface, Arsenale; bottom right: Byzantine chalice, Basilica di San Marco

Introduction

Every visitor discovers his or her own Venice, one of Europe's most beloved destinations, so open yourself to the magic of unknown streets and waterways, and their stories will become yours.

Venice runs on its historic canal system—vaporettos and gondolas crisscrossing the city's six *sestieri*. Of course, you should spend some time in a boat, even if it's just a quick hop by water taxi, but walking is the best way to explore this maze of bell towers and grand palazzos rising from the water. Venice is faded and crumbling, yet majestic and proud—as if the city knows the captivating spell it casts on visitors.

Whenever I visit Venice—I've been coming since I was 19—I always start with an espresso in Piazza San Marco. From there, I wander over to the Rialto Bridge—the nearby Rialto Market bursts with fresh flavors and the best Italian ingredients. For lunch, I might head to Santa Croce and some of the city's top restaurants. By night I am still lured by a white peach bellini at Harry's Bar.

Tourists take a leisurely gondola ride on this tranquil stretch of the Rio dei Barcaroli in the heart of San Marco.

The way to get the most out of Venice is to make a list of places you want to see. Take this beautiful book, get inspired to plan your route, and expect to stumble upon many surprises along the way—places that you never would have mapped out. Venice is a city of endless intrigue. So put on your walking shoes and maybe I'll see you there, bellini in hand, as you become the latest visitor to fall under this breathtaking city's eternal spell.

Annie Fitzsimmons
Contributing Editor, National Geographic Traveler *magazine*

Visiting Venice

Venice's origins go back to ca. 1000 when it was little more than a collection of independent island settlements. By the 15th century, the Republic of Venice was the most powerful maritime and commercial center in western Europe. Today it is a city with a vibrant cultural scene that attracts some 20 million tourists a year.

Venice in a Nutshell

Built on a cluster of islands in a marshy lagoon in the Adriatic Sea, Venice is just 3 square miles (8 sq km) in size. With its complex network of at least 175 canals crossed by as many as 400 bridges, the city is riddled with narrow alleys, secret courtyards, twists, turns, and dead ends. Each of the city's six neighborhoods (*sestieri*) has an identity of its own. Hugging the banks of the Grand Canal, San Marco and San Polo are the city's ancient administrative and mercantile centers. North of San Polo, Cannaregio was once home to the Jewish population; Santa Croce to the west has Venice's finest churches. Southwest of San Marco, Dorsoduro is known for its art; to the east, Castello was once the city's maritime hub.

Visiting the Sites of Venice Day-by-Day

Open every day With some exceptions for major public holidays, almost all sites are open every day.

Monday All sites open except Ca' Pesaro, Fondaco dei Turchi, La Pietà, Museo di Torcello, Palazzo Mocenigo, Palazzo Querini Stampalia, Scuola Grande di San Marco, and VizioVirtù Cioccolateria

Tuesday All sites open except Ca' Rezzonico, Collezione Peggy Guggenheim, Palazzo Grassi, Punta della Dogana

Wednesday All sites open

Thursday All sites open

Friday All sites open

Saturday All sites open except Arsenale and Museo Ebraico

Sunday All sites open except Arsenale, Chiesa dei Gesuati, Chiesa di San Giacomo dall'Orio, Chiesa di Santa Maria Formosa, Gianni Basso, Mercato di Rialto, Museo Storico Navale, and Scuola Grande di San Marco

Looking for bargains at a flea market in the Campo dei Frari

Navigating Venice

You can reach all major sights on foot and, outside of the San Marco/Rialto areas, the city is relatively crowd-free. But be warned—Venice is notoriously difficult to navigate. The many canals and bridges can be disorienting and you will get lost without a reliable map (available free from most hotels). This is all part of the experience, however, so just relax and go with the flow. Venice is entirely car-free, and locals rely on a waterbus service to get around. The most common mode of transport is the vaporetto, operating on at least 15 routes around the city.

Enjoying Venice for Less

There are several discount schemes to take advantage of during your stay. The most extensive is the **Venezia Unica** (see p. 176) city pass. Valid for seven days, this gives you free or discounted admission to many sights without waiting in line. You can even tailor the card to your itinerary, adding more sights, transportation, Wi-Fi, even public toilets. If this pass exceeds your needs, alternatives include the **Tourist Travel Card** (see p. 175), the Venice **Museum Pass** (see p. 176), and the **Chorus Pass** for churches (see p. 176).

Using This Guide

Each tour—which might be only a walk, or might also take advantage of the city's public transportation—is plotted on a map and has been planned to take into account opening hours and the times of day when sites are less crowded. Many end near restaurants or lively nightspots for evening activities.

Whirlwind Tours

Whirlwind Tours are for people who have only a day or weekend to spend in the city and want to be sure that they see the very best. Choose your tour based on your time and interests: One Day; Weekend; For Fun; Along the Grand Canal; For Art Lovers; For Foodies; and With Kids.

Tips For the Day and Weekend Tours, a Tips spread following the itinerary map provides insider information on detours from the key sites, extra places to see, nearby cafés and restaurants, and ideas for adapting the tours to suit your interests.

Site Descriptions

In the For Fun, Along the Grand Canal, For Art Lovers, For Foodies, and With Kids tours, key sites spreads following the maps provide descriptions of all the sites and necessary practical information for visitors.

Neighborhood Tours

The six neighborhood tours each begin with an introduction, followed by an itinerary map highlighting the key sites that make up the tour and detailed key sites descriptions. Each tour is followed by an "in-depth" spread showcasing one major site along the route, a "distinctly" Venice spread providing background information on a quintessential element of that neighborhood, and a "best of" spread that groups sites thematically.

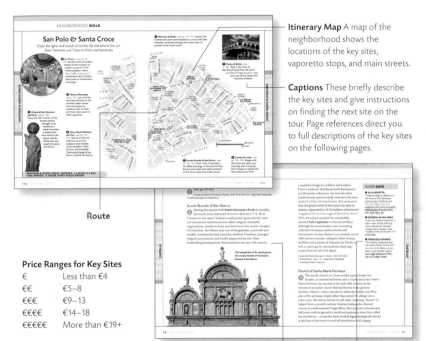

Itinerary Map A map of the neighborhood shows the locations of the key sites, vaporetto stops, and main streets.

Captions These briefly describe the key sites and give instructions on finding the next site on the tour. Page references direct you to full descriptions of the key sites on the following pages.

Route

Price Ranges for Key Sites

€	Less than €4
€€	€5–8
€€€	€9–13
€€€€	€14–18
€€€€€	More than €19+

Price Ranges for Good Eats (for one person, excluding drinks)

€	Less than €15
€€	€15–25
€€€	€25–45
€€€€	€45–60
€€€€€	More than €60

Key Sites Descriptions These provide a detailed description and highlights for each site, following the order on the map, plus its address, phone number, entrance fee, days closed, nearest vaporetto stop, and website address.

Good Eats Refer to these lists for a selection of cafés and restaurants along the tour.

PART 1

Whirlwind Tours

Venice in a Day

Explore Venice from the air, the water, and on the ground with this action-packed tour of the city's must-see sights.

7 Ca' d'Oro (see p. 98) Admire the view of the Grand Canal from the balcony of one of the city's finest palaces. From the Ca' d'Oro dock, clamber onto a vaporetto (line 1) headed back down the Grand Canal to San Marco-Vallaresso and walk a few yards on Calle Vallaresso.

6 Ponte di Rialto (see p. 114) Cross the fabled Rialto Bridge and follow the bend in the Grand Canal. From the quay at Mercato di Rialto, climb aboard a traditional wooden *traghetto* and pay the gondolier €2 to row across the Grand Canal.

5 Gallerie dell'Accademia (see pp. 140–143) From Byzantine to baroque, this collection of Venetian creations is one of Europe's greatest. From the dock near the museum entrance, hop onto a vaporetto (line 1 or 2) along the Grand Canal to Rialto "C" stop.

4 Zattere (see p. 136) Grab a bite to eat in one of the alfresco cafés along this popular promenade before heading inland on Rio Terra Foscarini.

San Marcuola
Casinò
Canal Grande
Riva de Biasio
CAMPO
SAN GIACOMO
DALL'ORIO
CAMPO
SAN
STIN
SAN
CAMPO
SAN POLO
CAMPO
DEI FRARI
San Tomà *Canal Grande*
Sant'Angelo
CAMPO
SANTA
MARGHERITA
Rio di Ca' Foscari
San
Samuele CAMPO
SAN
SAMUELE CAMPO
SANTO
STEFANO
CAMPO
SAN
BARNABA Ca' Rezzonico
DORSODURO
Accademia
PONTE DELL'
ACCADEMIA
**Gallerie
dell'Accademia 5**
Zattere
Zattere
4
Canale della Giudecca
FONDAMENTA

**VENICE IN A DAY DISTANCE: APPROX. 5 MILES (8 KM)
TIME: APPROX. 9 HOURS START: PIAZZA SAN MARCO**

WHIRLWIND TOURS

8 Harry's Bar (see p. 17) **Complete your day with a Bellini cocktail (if your wallet can take the hit) in the city's most renowned bar. Linger all evening or return to Piazza San Marco via the waterfront Riva degli Schiavoni.**

1 Basilica di San Marco (see pp. 64–65) **See Byzantine-style frescoes, stunning mosaics, and plundered treasures inside this magnificent church. Turn left out of the front doors and pass beneath the Campanile as you cross the Piazzetta San Marco en route to the waterfront.**

2 Palazzo Ducale (see pp. 66–67) Home to the supreme ruler of Venice for more than 400 years, the Doge's Palace is a Gothic masterpiece filled with treasures. Saunter over to the first vaporetto stop to the east of the palace and hop on a vaporetto (line 2) across the Bacino di San Marco.

3 Campanile di San Giorgio Maggiore (see p. 90) **Ride the elevator to the top of the campanile for a vertigo-inducing view across Venice and the lagoon. Hop back onto a vaporetto (line 2), this time headed for the Zattere.**

Fondamente Nove

San Stae

STRADA NOVA

CANNAREGIO

Rio dei Gesuiti

FONDAMENTE NOVE

7 Ca' d'Oro

Ca' d'Oro

CAMPO DEI SANTI APOSTOLI

Rio dei Mendicanti

CAMPO BECCARIE

Mercato di Rialto

Rialto Mercato

CAMPO SANTI GIOVANNI E PAOLO

di San Cassiano

POLO

CAMPO SAN GIACOMO DI RIALTO

6 Ponte di Rialto

Rialto

CAMPO SANTA MARIA FORMOSA

San Silvestro

CASTELLO

CAMPO SAN LUCA

CAMPO MANIN

SAN MARCO

CAMPO SAN GALLO

Bacino Orseolo

PIAZZA SAN MARCO

Basilica di San Marco

CAMPO SAN ZACCARIA

CAMPO SANT' ANGELO

1

2 Palazzo Ducale

CAMPO SAN MAURIZIO

Campanile di San Marco

San Zaccaria

Harry's Bar **8**

GIARDINI EX REALI

San Marco

Santa Maria del Giglio

Salute

Bacino di San Marco

Collezione Peggy Guggenheim

Punta della Dogana

ISOLA DI SAN GIORGIO MAGGIORE

San Giorgio

3

DELLE ZATTERE

Spirito Santo

0 ___ 400 meters
0 ___ 400 yards

Campanile di San Giorgio Maggiore

Tips

For those who have only one day to explore the Queen of the Adriatic, this tour combines the best of Venice's many historic and cultural sights. Cross-references lead to detailed information on each of them, and you can read on below for time-saving tips, historic eateries, and suggestions for alternatives.

❶ **Basilica di San Marco** (see pp. 64–65) First thing in the morning is the best time to visit this mind-blowing pastiche of domes, spires, arches, and columns. An even better tip is to arrive in time for a sung Mass (*7 a.m., 8 a.m., 9 a.m. weekdays, Sun.*) before the church opens to the public, when there are far fewer people about. Alternatively, if lines are long and the aisles already packed, admire the facade over an espresso in one of the outdoor cafés in the piazza.

❷ **Palazzo Ducale** (see pp. 66–67) If the Doge's Palace is overcrowded, focus your visit on the ■ SALA DEL MAGGIOR CONSIGLIO (Grand Council Chamber), the opulent ■ STATE APARTMENTS, and the notorious ■ PRIGIONI (Prisons). Be sure to go inside to sneak a peak at the ■ PONTE DEI SOSPIRI (Bridge of Sighs) from Ponte della Paglia on the waterfront.

❸ **Campanile di San Giorgio Maggiore** (see p. 90) This bell tower on ■ ISOLA DI SAN GIORGIO MAGGIORE offers the best view in Venice. If pushed for time, head up the soaring ■ CAMPANILE DI SAN MARCO (see p. 59) instead, before leaving the piazza.

❹ **Zattere** (see p. 136) The lively outdoor cafés and waterfront restaurants of this popular promenade provide a perfect spot to grab lunch (see Good Eats p. 138). For ice cream, head to ■ GELATERIA NICO (*Fondamenta Zattere al Ponte Longo, 041 522 5293*), proudly serving Venetians with its specialty praline and cream flavor since 1937.

❺ **Gallerie dell'Accademia** (see pp. 140–143) The chronological arrangement of this former art academy allows you to visit just one or two periods from the Byzantine and

Capturing the scene in St. Mark's Square

Gothic through the Renaissance and baroque eras. If religious art isn't your thing, visit the ■ COLLEZIONE PEGGY GUGGENHEIM (see p. 135) instead, a fabulous assemblage of modern art that's just a short walk down the same side of the Grand Canal.

❻ Ponte di Rialto (see p. 114) You might just be in time to catch the last calls of the market traders at the ■ MERCATO DI RIALTO (Rialto Market; see pp. 114–115). If you didn't lunch along the ■ ZATTERE, the Rialto area is rife with such ancient watering holes as ■ DO MORI *(Calle Do Mori, 041 522 5401, closed Sun., €€)*, a time-warp tavern founded in 1462 and allegedly the city's oldest wine bar *(bacaro)*. Slip into any one of them for a late bite.

❼ Ca' d'Oro (see p. 98) Duck into the 15th-century House of Gold for

works by Mantegna, Carpaccio, Titian, and other Renaissance masters. Instead of taking a vaporetto to ■ PIAZZA SAN MARCO return to the Rialto Market area by traghetto *(€)*. Stroll back across the Ponte di Rialto for an in-depth introduction to Italian wine at ■ ENOTECA MILLEVINI (see p. 41) and nearby neighborhood bars.

❽ Harry's Bar *(Calle Vallaresso 1323, 041 528 5777, €€€)* Founded in 1931 by Giuseppe Cipriani—with money loaned to him by young American Harry Pickering—this atmospheric hidey-hole is a Venetian institution. Extend your whirlwind day into the evening with a blend of comedy and history at an event called ■ VENEZIA THE SHOW (see p. 49). This long-running show at the Teatro San Gallo combines live acting with video projections.

CUSTOMIZING **YOUR DAY**

If you've no head for heights, skip Campanile di San Giorgio and take a vaporetto to nearby Giudecca island. You'll find plenty to explore, including such landmarks as the 16th-century **Chiesa del Santissimo Redentore** (see p. 90) and the **Mariano Fortuny** fabric factory and showroom (see p. 90). Take the vaporetto from Redentore to Zattere to resume the walk.

Venice in a Weekend

A tour of the city's most iconic sights from the Piazza San Marco to the Grand Canal ends with a romantic walk on the waterfront.

❻ Zattere (see p. 136) Round out your day with supper at one of the waterfront restaurants on this popular evening promenade.

❺ Scuola Grande di San Rocco (see pp. 122–125) It took Tintoretto nearly **20 years** to create this Venetian version of the Sistine Chapel, grandest of all the grand schools. Make your way to Campo Santa Margherita and along the Carmini and San Sebastiano canals to the Zattere.

❹ Mercato di Rialto (see pp. 114–115) Browse the stalls of this ancient market. Amble across the Ponte di Rialto and catch a vaporetto (line 1 or 2) from Rialto "C" pier. Alighting at San Tomà, stroll Calle del Traghetto northwest toward Campo San Rocco.

RIO TERRA FARSETTI

San Marcuola
Casinò

Canal Grande

RIO TERRA LISTA
DI SPAGNA

PONTE
D. SCALZI

Riva de
Biasio

Ferrovia
Scalzi

Rio Marin

CAMPO
SAN GIACOMO
DALL'ORIO

Ferrovia
Santa Lucia

PONTE DELLA
COSTITUZIONE

GIARDINO
PAPADÓPOLI

CAMPO D.
TOLENTINI

CAMPO
SAN
STIN

S A N

CAMPO
SAN POLO

S A N T A
C R O C E

Scuola Grande
di San Rocco **❺**

CAMPO
DEI FRARI

Rio Nuovo

Rio di Ca' Fóscari

San Tomà

Sant'Angelo

CAMPO
SANTA
MARGHERITA

San
Samuele

CAMPO
SAN
SAMUELE

CAMPO
SANTO
STEFANO

CAMPO SAN
BARNABA

Ca' Rezzonico

D O R S O D U R O

Accademia

PONTE DELL'
ACCADEMIA

FONDAMENTA ZATTERE AL PONTE LUNGO

San
Basilio

Rio di San Trovaso

Chiesa
dei Gesuati

Canale della Giudecca

Zattere

❻

Zattere

FONDAMENTA

❶ Basilica di San Marco (see pp. 64–65) Admire the grandiloquent facade and stroll through the richly decorated interior of Venice's landmark church. Take the few steps across the Piazzetta San Marco to the Doge's Palace.

❷ Palazzo Ducale (see pp. 66–67) Book yourself a place on the Secret Itinerary tour at the Doge's Palace. Saunter over to the first vaporetto stop (line 1) to the east of the palace and cruise up the Grand Canal to the Ca' d'Oro dock.

❸ Ca' d'Oro (see p. 98) Marvel at this palace's lavish interior decoration. Follow Calle Ca' d'Oro and Strada Nova around the block to Campo Santa Sofia, where ferrymen will row you across the canal to the Rialto district in a traditional wooden traghetto.

Tips

Two days provide enough time to immerse yourself in Venice's architecture, art, and nightlife without getting exhausted. Day One covers the city's major sights, with plenty of scope for improvisation. Read about the main attractions later in the book and consider the following tips for interesting alternatives.

❶ **Basilica di San Marco** (see pp. 64–65) If you can't face the crowds at St. Mark's Basilica, rise above them with a climb up the ■ CAMPANILE (see p. 59), the city's landmark bell tower. Alternatively, head to the relative calm of the adjacent ■ BACINO ORSEOLO (Orseolo Basin; see p. 60), chockablock with gondolas coming and going. This is, perhaps, the best place in the city to photograph the lovely wooden boats.

❷ **Palazzo Ducale** (see pp. 66–67), At the opposite end of the piazza, the ■ MUSEO CORRER (Correr Museum; see p. 60) makes a good alternative to the Doge's Palace if jostling with tourists doesn't appeal. Aspects of Venetian history are illuminated inside the grandiose apartments that Napoleon transformed into his residence after the late 18th-century French conquest of Venice.

❸ **Ca' d'Oro** (see p. 98) Instead of admiring the Renaissance artwork inside the House of Gold, venture deeper into the ■ CANNAREGIO district. A stroll on Strada Nova and Fondamenta San Felice takes you to the ■ FONDAMENTA DELLA MISERICORDIA (see pp. 96–97), a canalside walkway flanked by old houses, restaurants, wine bars, and sidewalk cafés. Linger here for lunch or a refreshing drink. (see Good Eats, p. 96).

❹ **Mercato di Rialto** (see pp. 114–115) Before slipping into the helter-skelter Rialto Market, step onto Antonio da Ponte's sublime ■ PONTE DI RIALTO (see p. 114), which leaps the water in a single bound between the neighborhoods of San Marco and San Polo. The market has two main areas—the Pescheria (fish market) and Erberia (fruit and vegetable market). The photo opportunities are fantastic.

Chilling in Campo Santa Margherita

❺ Scuola Grande di San Rocco (see pp. 122–125) You might feel that the weather is just too lovely for indoors, in which case this *scuola* is less than a 20-minute walk from some of Venice's most intriguing squares. With afternoon fading, make your way via San Pantalon bridge to ■ CAMPO SANTA MARGHERITA (see p. 139), with its food and clothing stalls, buskers, and bars frequented by students from the nearby universities. It's just a few steps more down the Rio Terà Canal to the ■ PONTE DEI PUGNI (see p. 148), where rival families engaged in pugilistic rites that had the losers tossed into the canal. The adjacent ■ CAMPO SAN BARNABA (see p. 148) offers another place to rest your legs and contemplate the architecture. From there it's another short walk via Fondamenta di Borgo and Fondamenta Bonlini to the ■ CAMPO SAN TROVASO (see p. 88) and

its splendid Renaissance church. The Alpine-looking structure over to one side of the campo is the ■ SQUERO DI SAN TROVASO (see p. 89), an ancient boatyard where many of the city's gondolas are repaired and new ones constructed. Also close at hand is ■ VITRARIA GLASS +A MUSEUM (see p. 89), inside the 16th-century Palazzo Nani Mocenigo.

❻ Zattere (see p. 136) If you skipped the Scuola Grande di San Rocco earlier in the day, you still have your chance to see a Tintoretto masterpiece at the somewhat calmer ■ CHIESA DEI GESUATI (see p. 137). The artist's "Crucifixion" may steal the show, but don't allow it to distract you from the rococo ceiling frescoes by Tiepolo. Finish with a spritz at ■ EL CHIOSCHETTO (see p. 72), a little waterfront bar on the Zattere.

CUSTOMIZING **YOUR DAY**

Skip Ca' d'Oro and head instead to the old Jewish **Ghetto** (see pp. 102–103). Although the city's Jewish population is now dispersed throughout Venice, the **Campo del Ghetto Nuovo** is still a hub of Jewish organizations and businesses. In addition to telling the story of the city's Jews, the nearby **Museo Ebraico** offers guided tours of the neighborhood (available in English).

Venice in a Weekend

Journey through more than one thousand years of local and global art and cap your day off with a classic night on the town.

❶ **Collezione Peggy Guggenheim** (see p. 135) **Make your way along Calle del Bastion and Campiello Barbaro to this mansion on the Grand Canal. After eyeballing the Picassos and Pollocks, continue west on Calle della Chiesa, then Piscina Forner, and north on Rio Terrà Foscarini to another great art collection.**

❷ **Gallerie dell'Accademia** (see pp. 140–143) From Byzantine and baroque, a thousand years of Venetian art cover the walls of this epic art museum. From the pier outside the museum, board a vaporetto (line 1) bound for Ferrovia.

❸ **Grand Canal Cruise** (see pp. 30–33) Admire the splendid palaces and warehouses arrayed along the entire length of the city's most celebrated waterway. On reaching the Ferrovia stop (in front of Santa Lucia Station) hop off and board another vaporetto (line 1) headed back along the Grand Canal.

VENICE IN A WEEKEND DAY 2   DISTANCE: APPROX. 4.5 MILES (7 KM) TIME: APPROX. 8–9 HOURS   VAPORETTO START: SALUTE

WHIRLWIND TOURS

5 **Piazza San Marco by Night** (see p. 25) Quaff cocktails at Harry's Bar, listen to live music at the Caffè Florian, and then join the night owls at Caffè Centrale before wending your way home through the sleeping city.

4 **Ca' Rezzonico** (see p. 138) Revel in the decadence of 18th-century Venice in a palace museum still decorated as if the original inhabitants had never left. Jump back onto a vaporetto (line 1) bound for San Marco.

Map labels:

Ca' d'Oro
CAMPO DELLA PESCHERIA
Rialto Mercato
CAMPO DEI SANTI APOSTOLI
CAMPO SAN GIACOMO DI RIALTO
PONTE DI RIALTO
Rialto
San Silvestro
CORTE SECONDA DEL MILION
Fondaco dei Tedeschi
CAMPO SANTI GIOVANNI E PAOLO
CAMPO SANTA MARIA FORMOSA
CASTELLO
CAMPO SAN LUCA
CAMPO MANIN
SAN MARCO
Bacino Orseolo
Piazza San Marco
Basilica di San Marco
Palazzo Ducale
CAMPO SAN ZACCARIA
Teatro La Fenice
Campanile di San Marco
PIAZZETTA SAN MARCO
San Zaccaria
GIARDINI EX REALI
San Marco
Bacino di San Marco
Canale di San Marco
Salute
Punta della Dogana
Santa Maria della Salute

Tips

Day Two in Venice revolves around art and the world-class museums arrayed along the Grand Canal. But once again, there are plenty of opportunities to go off script if you don't feel like spending most of your day indoors. Use the page references provided to discover detours along the way.

DAY 2

❶ Collezione Peggy Guggenheim (see p. 135) Salute vaporetto pier is the jumping-off point for other sights on the Dorsoduro peninsula. Before going anywhere, stop to look at the view. The peninsula comes to a dramatic end here and offers one of the best views of the San Marco shoreline and across the water to San Giorgio and Giudecca islands. If you do one thing at the Peggy Guggenheim Collection, visit the

Collezione Peggy Guggenheim

■ NASHER SCULPTURE GARDEN, filled with surrealist art and curious installations. The cool café here is a good spot for light refreshments. Alternatively, replace the Guggenheim with a visit to the ■ PUNTA DELLA DOGANA (Museum of Contemporary Art; see p. 137), where French tycoon François-Henri Pinault showcases part of his vast and impressive collection.

❷ Gallerie dell'Accademia (see pp. 140–143) Make time to step into ■ SANTA MARIA DELLA SALUTE (see pp. 134–135), which looms above the floating dock. This is one of the city's glorious plague churches built to thank the Virgin Mary for ridding Venice of the Black Death. Behind the soaring white stone facade—inspired by a Roman triumphal arch—the octagonal church is flush with Catholic symbolism and bold devotional art. If you're hungry, zip across the water for a relaxed buffet lunch before starting your canal tour. ■ **Palazzo Franchetti** (*Campo Santo Stefano, 041 240 7711, closed Sat., Sun., €€, palazzofranchetti.it*) has a small budget café with vast windows overlooking a garden.

❸ Grand Canal Cruise (see pp. 30–33) The beauty of the Grand Canal cruise is that you can hop off and on whenever you want. Tailor your cruise to suit both the time you have and your interests. You'll see 20th-century painting and sculpture inside the ■ **Ca' Pesaro** (see pp. 116–117), the 17th-century palace that now houses the eclectic works of the Galleria Internazionale d'Arte Moderna. If you're looking for souvenirs, you'll find exquisite Italian wares at the ■ **Fondaco dei Tedeschi** (see pp. 62–63) shopping emporium. Or pop into 13th-century ■ **Fondaco dei Turchi** (see p. 49) where dinosaur bones and butterfly collections highlight a natural history museum that also features an aquarium filled with Adriatic marine life.

❹ Ca' Rezzonico (see p. 138) If you've missed out on the Punta della Dogana, skip Ca' Rezzonico, and head instead to the 18th-century ■ **Palazzo**

Grassi (see p. 62), with another substantial cache of Pinault's massive modern art collection. The exhibition space by Japanese architect Tadao Ando is worth a visit in its own right.

❺ Piazza San Marco by Night The San Marco area (see pp. 58–63) offers plenty of ways to extend your evening with a splash of Venetian performing arts. ■ **Teatro La Fenice** (see p. 61) runs an impressive schedule of opera and symphony through most of the year. Vivaldi's *Four Seasons* is performed in full 18th-century costume at the ■ **Scuola Grande di San Teodoro** (see p. 72). ■ **Musica a Palazzo** (see p. 29) has "progressive" opera, the audience following along and mingling with the actors and musicians as performances move from room to room in the waterfront Palazzo Barbarigo Minotto.

CUSTOMIZING **YOUR DAY**

Replace one of the Dorsoduro sights with some fun at **Ca' Macana** (see p. 44). This ancient mask-making outfit offers one- and two-hour workshops during which participants learn eight different techniques to decorate two of their own papier-mâché masks. Families and small children are welcome. The workshop is about a six-minute walk from the Gallerie dell'Accademia.

Venice for Fun

Bypass the milling crowds on this carefree day of shopping, drinking, eating, and opera.

❽ Caffè Centrale (see p. 29) Enjoy a nightcap and after-opera munchies at this hip, contemporary cocktail lounge.

❼ Musica a Palazzo (see p. 29) Join other enthusiasts for an offbeat opera performance. After the bravos, zigzag northeast via Campiello Traghetto and Calle Veste to Calle Drio la Chiesa.

❻ Bar Longhi (see p. 29) Sip pretheater cocktails in the lounge of The Gritti Palace hotel. It's a short stroll via the Campiello Traghetto, Ponte Duodo o Barbarigo, and Fondamenta Duodo o Barbarigo to reach the opera.

**FOR FUN DISTANCE: APPROX. 8 MILES (13 KM)
TIME: APPROX. 9 HOURS START: PIAZZA SAN MARCO**

❶ Chic San Marco (see p. 28)
Browse the chic boutiques west of
Piazza San Marco. From San Marco del
Giglio dock, hop on a vaporetto (line 1)
across the Grand Canal to Salute and
follow Calle del Bastion.

❷ Venetia Studium (see p. 28) Admire
the high-class wares in this emporium of
Venetian design. Make your way back to
the Salute dock and hop on a vaporetto
(line 1) bound for San Zaccaria. Stroll
east on Riva degli Schiavoni to the
Hotel Metropole.

❸ High Tea at the Met (see p. 28)
Take a time trip back to 19th-century
Venice during afternoon tea at the
Metropole. Right beside the Met, head
north on Calle de la Pietà and then east
on Salizada dei Greci.

❹ Venice Gallery (see p. 28) This
offbeat shop hawks art created by local
artist Gianfranco Missiaja. Cross the
Ponte dei Greci and follow Fondamenta
San Lorenzo north. Head west on Calle
San Lorenzo and north on Calle de la
Madoneta to reach the bookshop.

❺ Libreria Acqua Alta (see pp. 28–29)
Browse the shelves—and bathtubs—of this
quirky bookshop. Zigzag from Calle Tetta
to Calle Cappuccine Castello to reach the
Ospedale dock. Take a vaporetto (line 5.1)
to Santa Maria del Giglio.

Map labels:
Rio dei Mendicanti
Ospedale
CAMPO SANTI GIOVANNI E PAOLO
Rio di Santa Giustina
Celestia
CAMPO DELLA CONFRATERNITA
CAMPO SANTA MARIA FORMOSA
❺ Libreria Acqua Alta
CAMPO SAN LORENZO
C A S T E L L O
❹ Venice Gallery
Arsenale
CAMPO SAN ZACCARIA
Basilica di San Marco
Palazzo Ducale
❸ The Metropole
RIVA DEGLI SCHIAVONI
San Zaccaria
Arsenale
di Marco
Canale di San Marco
Giardini della Biennale Internazionale d'Arte
ISOLA DI SAN GIORGIO MAGGIORE
San Giorgio

0   400 meters
0   400 yards

WHIRLWIND TOURS

WHIRLWIND TOURS

Chic San Marco

1 Browse the chic boutiques around **Piazza San Marco** (see pp. 58–59). **The Merchant of Venice** (*Campo San Fantin 1895, 041 296 0559, closed Mon., themerchantofvenice.it*) is an atmospheric perfumery located in an old pharmacy. **Il Prato** (*Calle delle Ostreghe 2456/9, 041 523 1148, ilpratovenezia.com*) specializes in authentic Venetian glassware, jewelry, and luxury leather items.

Piazza San Marco and environs • Vaporetto: San Marco, Santa Maria del Giglio

Venetia Studium

2 In addition to its own brand of furnishings and accessories, this high-end store showcases Fortuny silk and glass lamps.

Calle del Bastion 180/a • 041 523 6953 • Vaporetto: Salute • venetiastudium.com

High Tea at the Met

3 This afternoon ritual is staged in collaboration with Dammann Frères, the venerable French tea company, founded in1925. The service includes handmade pastries and a selection of world teas.

Riva degli Schiavoni 4149 • 041 520 5044 • Vaporetto: San Zaccaria • €€€€€
• hotelmetropole.com

Venice Gallery

4 The works of Venetian artist and architect Gianfranco Missiaja and his students are on display at this hidden-away gallery. The selection includes colorful city scenes, commedia dell'arte carnival characters, abstracts, and papier-mâché statuettes.

Salizada dei Greci 3456 • 041 523 4343 • Vaporetto: San Zaccaria • venicegallery.it

Libreria Acqua Alta

5 Books are displayed in old bathtubs, wheelbarrows, and even a gondola in this eccentric bookstore that backs onto a canal.

As the name suggest (*acqua alta* means "high water" in Italian), the shop is not immune to flooding. One of the staircases is even made from books damaged in some past deluge.

Calle Longa Santa Maria Formosa 5176/B
• 041 296 0841 • Vaporetto: Ospedale

Bar Longhi

6 Hemingway is one of the many celebrities who have wet their whistles at The Gritti Palace hotel marble bar. During the summer, grab a seat on the waterfront terrace.

Campo Santa Maria del Giglio • 041 794 611
• €€ • Vaporetto: Santa Maria del Giglio
• thegrittipalace.com

Musica a Palazzo

7 The Palazzo Barbarigo Minotto provides a spectacular setting for an evening of "progressive" Italian opera, with each act staged in a different room of the sumptuously decorated baroque palace. *La Traviata, Rigoletto,* and *The Barber of Seville* are performed on different nights each week, so why not actually attend Musica a Palazzo more than once?

Fondamenta Duodo o Barbarigo 2504 • 340 971 7272 • €€€€€ • Vaporetto: Santa Maria del Giglio • www.musicapalazzo.com

Caffè Centrale

8 The perfect spot for a nightcap after the opera. Sip a late-night Negroni cocktail or Tiramisu Martini before heading to bed.

Calle Piscina de Frezzaria 1659/B • 041 887 6642 • €€ • Vaporetto: San Marco, Santa Maria del Giglio, Sant'Angelo • caffecentralevenezia.com

A staircase made of books at Castello's Libreria Acqua Alta bookstore leads to a view overlooking the canal.

Along the Grand Canal

Spend the day cruising the Grand Canal. Admire the waterfront facades and stop off here and there for a burst of culture.

❽ Ca' d'Oro
(see pp. 33, 98)
No longer shimmering with gold, this building remains an impressive example of Renaissance architecture nevertheless.

❼ Ca' Loredan (see p. 33)
Venice's city hall occupies a 14th-century palace later modified by the aristocratic Loredan family.

❻ Palazzo Grassi (see pp. 33, 62)
Admire the classical Venetian charm of this palace turned art gallery.

❺ Ca' Rezzonico (see pp. 33, 138)
The focus of this riverside museum is the opulence of 18th-century Venice.

San Marcuola Casinò

CAMPO SAN GIACOMO DALL'ORIO

PIAZZALE ROMA

GIARDINO PAPADÓPOLI

CAMPO D. TOLENTINI

CAMPO SAN STIN

CAMPO SAN POLO

SANTA CROCE

Santa Maria Gloriosa dei Frari

CAMPO DEI FRARI

Rio Nuovo

San Tomà

Rio di Ca' Foscari

Palazzo Mocenigo

CAMPO SANTA MARGHERITA

❻ Palazzo Grassi

Ca' Rezzonico ❺

San Samuele

CAMPO SANTO STEFANO

Ca' Rezzonico

DORSODURO

PONTE DELL' ACCADEMIA

Accademia

Gallerie dell' Accademia

**ALONG THE GRAND CANAL   DISTANCE: APPROX. 1.8 MILES (3 KM)
TIME: APPROX. 8 HOURS   START: PIAZZA SAN MARCO**

WHIRLWIND TOURS

9 Ca' Pesaro (see pp. 33, 116–117) **Kandinsky and Klimt, Moore and Matisse are among the masters on display inside this 17th-century palace, now home to the Museum of Modern Art.**

1 Ca' Giustinian (see p. 32) **Hop onto a line N or line 1 vaporetto near Piazza San Marco and start your cruise up the Grand Canal past Ca' Giustinian, a Gothic masterpiece.**

2 The Gritti Palace (see p. 32) **Once a Gothic palace, now a hotel. Enter the public rooms to see Murano mirrors and antique damask upholstery.**

3 Ca' Dario (see p. 32) **Immortalized by Monet, this 15th-century palace stages the occasional art exhibition.**

4 Collezione Peggy Guggenheim (see pp. 32, 135) **Now a modern art gallery, only the first floor of this 18th-century palace was ever built.**

Map labels:

CANNAREGIO

STRADA NOVA

Canale dello Misericordia

FONDAMENTE NOVE

Fondamente Nove

Rio dei Gesuiti

San Stae

Ca' Pesaro
9

Cassiano

Rio di San

CAMPO BECCARIE

8 Ca' d'Oro
Ca' d'Oro

CAMPO DEI SANTI APOSTOLI

Rialto Mercato

CAMPO SAN GIACOMO DI RIALTO

CORTE SECONDA DEL MILION

SAN POLO

PONTE DI RIALTO

Rialto

San Silvestro

CAMPO SANTA MARIA FORMOSA

Canal Grande

Sant'Angelo

7 Ca' Loredan

CAMPO SAN LUCA

CAMPO MANIN

Basilica di San Marco

CAMPO SANT' ANGELO

SAN MARCO

CAMPO SAN GALLO

Teatro La Fenice

Bacino Orseolo

PIAZZA SAN MARCO

Palazzo Ducale

PIAZZETTA SAN MARCO

CAMPO SAN MAURÍZIO

Campanile di San Marco

Ca' Giustinian
1

GIARDINI EX REALI

San Marco

The Gritti Palace
2

Santa Maria del Giglio

Salute

Bacino di San Marco

4 3 Ca' Dario

Punta della Dogana

Collezione Peggy Guggenheim

| 0 | 400 meters |
| 0 | 400 yards |

Ca' Giustinian

1 Headquarters of the **Biennale di Venezia** (Venice Biennale, see p. 82), this flamboyant four-story palace hugs the right bank just beyond the Palace Gardens. Erected in the 15th century, the palace provides a venue for various exhibitions and events.

San Marco 1364a • 041 521 8711 • Vaporetto: San Marco • labiennale.org

The Gritti Palace

2 Built for the wealthy Pisani clan in 1475, this splendid Renaissance palace has long been a hotel hosting A-list celebrities from Bogart and Bacall to Springsteen and Jagger.

Campo Santa Maria del Giglio 2467 • 041 794 611 • Vaporetto: Santa Maria del Giglio • thegrittipalace.com

Claude Monet's painting of Ca' Dario on the Grand Canal

Ca' Dario

3 Completed in the late 15th century, this privately owned palazzo sometimes stages public art exhibitions in conjunction with **Collezione Peggy Guggenheim.**

Campiello Barbaro • Vaporetto: Salute

Collezione Peggy Guggenheim

4 Named Palazzo Venier dei Leoni, for the lion heads that decorate its waterline wall, this 18th-century palace is now a fantastic modern art museum.

Calle della Chiesa 707 • 041 240 5411
• Closed Tues. • €€€€ • Vaporetto: Salute
• www.guggenheim-venice.it

Ca' Rezzonico

5 Among the highlights in this 18th-century palace are the ceiling frescoes of the **Nuptial Allegory Room,** an ancient pharmacy, and Longhi's satirical portraits.

Fondamenta Rezzonico 3136 • 041 241 0100 • Closed Tues. • €€€ • Vaporetto: Ca' Rezzonico • carezzonico.visitmuve.it

Palazzo Grassi

6 Switching focus to the right bank, this 18th-century waterfront palace is now a showcase for the modern art of French tycoon François-Henri Pinault. The rotating exhibits feature cutting-edge contemporary artists from around the globe.

Campo San Samuele • 041 271 9031 • closed Tues. • €€€ • Vaporetto: San Samuele • palazzograssi.it

Ca' Loredan

7 Originally built in the 14th century, the palace is home to City Hall. Civil weddings are conducted inside in a room decorated with Renaissance paintings and Murano glass chandeliers.

Calle Loredan 4122 • Vaporetto. Rialto

Ca' d'Oro

8 From the third-floor balcony, see if you can spot the marble relief of an elephant on the building's facade.

Calle Ca' d'Oro • 041 522 2349 • €€ • Vaporetto: Ca' d'Oro • cadoro.org

Ca' Pesaro

9 Venetian architectural maestro Baldassare Longhena designed this 17th-century palace for the Pesaro family. It now houses the Museum of Modern Art.

Fondamenta de Ca' Pesaro • 041 721 127 • €€€ • Closed Mon., Jan. 1, Dec. 25 • Vaporetto: San Stae • capesaro.visitmuve.it

Venice for Art Lovers

Bellini, Tiepolo, and Longhi are among the masters encountered on this artistic amble through this city's lesser-known churches and palaces.

❼ Zattere (see pp. 37, 136) **Stroll Dorsoduro's "Art Mile" and have drinks or dinner in one of the waterfront cafés.**

❻ Chiesa di Santa Maria dei Derelitti (see p. 37) This Andrea Palladio church is renowned for its magnificent Pietro Nacchini organ. A short walk north on Calle del Cafetier and Calle Cappuccine Castello takes you back to the waterfront. Board a vaporetto (line 5.1) to the Zattere.

❺ Palazzo Querini Stampalia (see p. 37) One of Europe's finest house museums showcases the everyday life of Venetian aristocrats during the Renaissance and baroque periods. After lunch in the museum café, return to Campo Santa Maria Formosa and follow Calle Longa Santa Maria Formosa and Calle Tetta.

**FOR ART LOVERS   DISTANCE: APPROX. 5 MILES (8 KM)
TIME: APPROX. 7–8 HOURS   START: PALAZZO MOCENIGO**

1 **Palazzo Mocenigo** (see pp. 36, 117) Venetian fashion, fabrics, and perfumes through the ages take center stage in this palace museum. Follow Salizada San Stae to the Grand Canal and catch a vaporetto (line 1 or N) to San Zaccaria. After disembarking, head east on the waterfront and then north onto Calle de la Pietà.

2 **Istituto Ellenico** (see p. 36) Admire the ancient Byzantine icons in this treasure chest of the Greek Orthodox faith. Cross the Ponte dei Greci and follow Campo San Provolo to Campo San Zaccaria and its eponymous church.

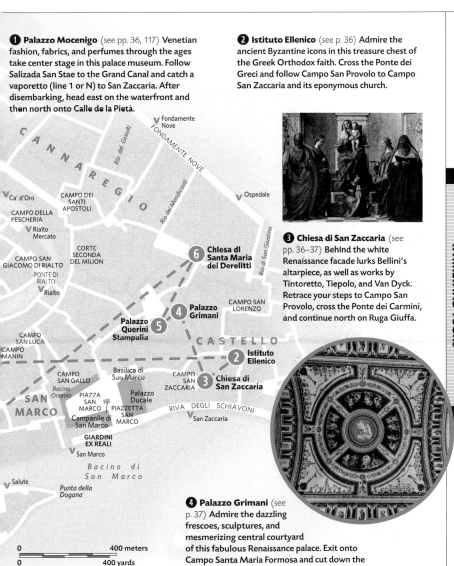

3 **Chiesa di San Zaccaria** (see pp. 36–37) Behind the white Renaissance facade lurks Bellini's altarpiece, as well as works by Tintoretto, Tiepolo, and Van Dyck. Retrace your steps to Campo San Provolo, cross the Ponte dei Carmini, and continue north on Ruga Giuffa.

4 **Palazzo Grimani** (see p. 37) Admire the dazzling frescoes, sculptures, and mesmerizing central courtyard of this fabulous Renaissance palace. Exit onto Campo Santa Maria Formosa and cut down the narrow lane on the southwest side.

Palazzo Mocenigo

1 Wearable art—of the tactile and aromatic variety—is the focus of this sumptuous palace museum in San Stae.

Fondamenta Mocenigo • 041 721 798 • €€ • Closed Mon., Jan. 1, Dec. 25 • Vaporetto: San Stae • mocenigo.visitmuve.it

Istituto Ellenico

2 Adjacent to the **Chiesa di San Giorgio dei Greci,** the Hellenic Institute Museum safeguards a rich collection of Byzantine icons, vestments, and other sacred objects.

Campo dei Greci • 041 522 6581 • € • Vaporetto: San Zaccaria • istitutoellenico.org

Chiesa di San Zaccaria

3 The facade of this medieval church is a spectacular blend of Gothic and Renaissance. The highlight within is Giovanni

The flooded crypt of Chiesa di San Zaccaria

Bellini's emotive altarpiece of the Virgin Mary with the Christ Child. Don't miss the flooded crypt, its tombs rising from the brown water.

Campo San Zaccaria • 041 522 1257 • € • Vaporetto: San Zaccaria

SAVVY **TRAVELER**

Travelers visiting multiple churches should buy a **Chorus Pass** (see p. 176), good for reduced admission into 18 Venetian churches.

Palazzo Grimani

4 This 16th-century palace is also well endowed with Renaissance frescoes and stuccowork. Camillo Mantovano's **Foliage Room** is a must-see, the ceiling covered in flora and fauna.

Ramo Grimani 4858 • 041 241 1507 • € • Closed Jan. 1, Dec. 25, May 1 • Vaporetto: San Zaccaria, Rialto, Ospedale • palazzogrimani.org

Palazzo Querini Stampalia

5 The everyday life of baroque Venice is the theme of this splendid palace museum, which flaunts period furnishings and fascinating scenes of masked balls, gambling dens, stick fights, and ball games by the likes of Pietro Longhi and Gabriele Bella.

Santa Maria Formosa 5252 • 041 271 1411 • Closed Mon. • €€€ • Vaporetto: San Zaccaria, Rialto • querinistampalia.org

Chiesa di Santa Maria dei Derelitti

6 Construction of this exquisite church started in 1575 under Andrea Palladio. The imposing Atlantes sculptures of the facade are by Flemish sculptor Josse de Corte.

Calle Barbaria de le Tole 6691 • 041 924 933 • € • Closed Sun.–Wed. • Vaporetto: Ospedale

Zattere

7 Highlights of Venice's unofficial "Art Mile" include the **Chiesa dei Gesuati** (see p. 137) and **Punta della Dogana** (see p. 137).

Fondamenta delle Zattere • Vaporetto: Zattere, San Basilio, Spirito Santo

Venice for Foodies

Freshly roasted coffee, exotic spices, fine wines, and cicchetti *are just a few of the treats along this gourmet trail through the old Rialto market area.*

1 **Mercato di Rialto** (see pp. 40, 114–115) **Arriving early in the morning, feast your eyes on the fish, fruit, and vegetables being off-loaded and sold at this ancient food market. Exit the market area via Ruga Vecchia San Giovanni and head south on Calle dei Cinque.**

C. DEL TINTOR

CAMPO S. MARIA
MATER DOMINI

CAMPO
S. BOLDO

C. DELL
AGNELLO

R. T. SECONDO

CAMPO
SANT'AGOSTIN

S A N
P O L O

C. PEZZANA

C. CORNER

CAMPO
SAN POLO

SALIZ. S.
POLO

3 **Drogheria Mascari** (see p. 40) Inhale the exotic aromas that emanate from Venice's last spice emporium. Having tantalized your taste buds, follow Calle San Mattia to Calle de le Do Spade and a choice of lunch spots.

2 **Caffè del Doge** (see p. 40) **Sip a freshly roasted cup of arabica or a dessert-like Giacometto. Retrace your steps on Ruga Vecchia San Giovanni and turn left on Ruga dei Spezieri.**

**FOR FOODIES   DISTANCE: APPROX. 0.6 MILES (1 KM)
TIME: APPROX. 7–8 HOURS   START: RIALTO MARKET**

WHIRLWIND TOURS

6 **Antiche Carampane** (see p. 41)
Venture deep into Rialto for a gourmet meal at this seafood restaurant.

V San Stae

CAMPO
SAN STAE

Canal

Ca' d'Oro

Ca' Pesaro

STRADA

Ca' d' Oro **V**

Grande

NOVA

C. D. REGINA

C. D. ROSA

CAMPO
SAN
CASSIANO

C. D. CAMPANILE

CALLE DEI BOTTERI

CAMPO D.
PESCHERIA

CAMPO
BECCARIE

**Drogheria
Mascari**

**Antiche
Carampane**

6

1 **Mercato
di Rialto**

V Rialto Mercato

4

3

**Cantina
Do Spade**

CAMPO
ERBERIA

CAMPIELLO
ALBRIZZI

R. VECCHIA S.

2

GIOVANNI

CAMPO
SANT'APONAL

C. D. STURION

**Caffè del
Doge**

5

**Enoteca
Millevini**

CAMPIELLO
MELONI

CAMPO SAN
SILVESTRO

RIVA DEL VIN

RIVA D. FERRO

Rialto **V**

C. TIEPOLO

V San Silvestro

RIVA DEL CARBON

CAMPO
SAN
SALVADOR

0   200 meters
0   200 yards

5 **Enoteca Millevini** (see p. 41)
Admire the vintage selection at this wine-tasting shop near the Fondaco dei Tedeschi and then linger over a spritz in one of the local bars. Cross the bridge back to the Rialto district, continue east on Riva del Vin and north on Calle della Madonna.

4 **Cantina Do Spade** (see p. 40)
Grab a light lunch at this time-warp eatery. Retrace your steps to Ruga dei Spezieri and follow it dead ahead across the Ponte di Rialto to Ramo del Fontego dei Tedeschi on the other side.

WHIRLWIND TOURS

IN **THE KNOW**

From **Enoteca Millevini**, it's a 10-minute walk to **Harry's Bar** (see p. 17), home to the iconic cocktail—the Bellini. Served in a champagne flute, the Bellini is puréed white peaches blended with prosecco, its pinkish color inspired by the toga of a saint painted by Venetian artist Giovanni Bellini.

Mercato di Rialto

1 Feast your eyes on the fresh fish, fruit, and vegetables of the Rialto Market.

Campo Cesare Battisti, Campo della Pescheria, and Campo Beccarie • Closed Sun. • Vaporetto: Rialto Mercato

Caffè del Doge

2 Rialto provided a venue for Europe's first coffeehouse in 1645, thanks to Venice's trading ties with the Ottoman Empire. Caffè del Doge serves fresh-roasted coffee and scrumptious coffee-based drinks like the Giacometto (with hazelnut chocolate, cream, and toasted hazelnuts).

Calle dei Cinque 609 • 041 522 7787 • € • Vaporetto: Rialto Mercato • caffedeldoge.com

Drogheria Mascari

3 Follow your nose down **Ruga dei Spezieri** ("Spice Alley") to the city's last spice emporium and a throwback to the days when Venice was a stop on the overland spice route from Asia. In addition to spices, the shop sells truffles, teas, and balsamic vinegar. There's also a good selection of Italian wines, jams, and marmalades.

Ruga dei Spezieri 381 • 041 522 9762 • Vaporetto: Rialto Mercato • imascari.com

Cantina Do Spade

4 The Rialto area is full of *bacari* (see pp. 106–109) in which Venetians gather for a drink, bite to eat, and neighborhood gossip. Besides good wine and spritz (Venice's signature summer drink), the bacari are renowned for *cicchetti*, the Venetian version of tapas. This, one of the oldest Rialto inns, serves deep-fried calamari, slivers of salted cod *(baccalà)*, tuna rissoles, and tiny meatballs.

Sotoportego de le Do Spade • 041 521 0583 • €€ • Vaporetto: Rialto Mercato • cantinadospade.com

Enoteca Millevini

On the San Marco side of the **Ponte di Rialto** (Rialto Bridge; see p. 114), this cozy wine-tasting store stocks an incredible array of Italian and foreign vintages. And the folks who run Millevini love sharing their knowledge with other oenophiles.

Ramo del Fontego dei Tedeschi 5362 • 041 520 6090 • €€ • Vaporetto: Rialto "C"

Antiche Carampane

Restaurants in the Rialto area are renowned for their fresh seafood dishes. The menu at Antiche Carampane is spangled with all sorts of maritime delights, from scampi and calamari to grilled fish and spaghetti in a spicy shellfish sauce.

Rio Terrà delle Carampane 1911 • 041 524 0165 • €€€€–€€€€€ • Vaporetto: Rialto Mercato, San Silvestro • antichecarampane.com

Shelves stacked with spices and countertops laden with cinnamon sticks at Drogheria Mascari

DAY
1

Venice in a Weekend With Kids

*Gondola rides and carnival masks, gelato and glassblowing—this tour
revolves around Venice's most endearing traditions.*

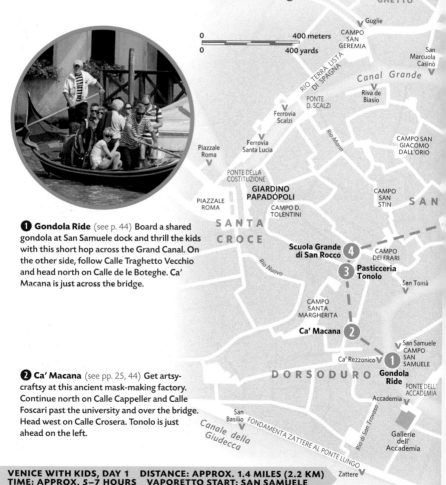

❶ Gondola Ride (see p. 44) **Board a shared
gondola at San Samuele dock and thrill the kids
with this short hop across the Grand Canal. On
the other side, follow Calle Traghetto Vecchio
and head north on Calle de le Boteghe. Ca'
Macana is just across the bridge.**

❷ Ca' Macana (see pp. 25, 44) **Get artsy-
craftsy at this ancient mask-making factory.
Continue north on Calle Cappeller and Calle
Foscari past the university and over the bridge.
Head west on Calle Crosera. Tonolo is just
ahead on the left.**

**VENICE WITH KIDS, DAY 1   DISTANCE: APPROX. 1.4 MILES (2.2 KM)
TIME: APPROX. 5–7 HOURS   VAPORETTO START: SAN SAMUELE**

6 Mauro Vianello (see p. 45) Your children will watch in wonder as Mauro turns molten glass into tiny sea creatures and other colorful animals.

5 Gelateria White (see p. 45) Treat the kids to a gelato or sorbet with the sauce or topping of their choice. Backtrack and head northwest on Ruga dei Spezieri and follow the zigzag path through Campo Beccarie and Campo San Cassiano to the glass factory.

4 Scuola Grande di San Rocco (see pp. 45, 122–125) Kids will get dizzy gazing at the ceilings. Follow Calle Tintoretto and Calle Larga Prima east, through Campo San Tomà, to San Tomà dock and take a vaporetto (line 1 or 2) to the Rialto "C" stop. Cross Ponte di Rialto and walk northwest on Ruga dei Oresi then southwest on Ruga Vecchia San Giovanni.

3 Pasticceria Tonolo (see p. 45) Enjoy a treat at this legendary Venetian bakery. Head west on Calle Crosera then north on Calle Fianco de la Scuola. Cross the wooden bridge and walk straight ahead into the Campo San Rocco.

Gondola Ride

1 Cross the Grand Canal in one of the traghetti (stand-up gondolas) from San Samuele to **Ca' Rezzonico** (see p. 138). Most of these wooden passenger boats are operated by gondoliers, who take it in turns. The crossing takes about five minutes.

Campo San Samuele • 041 520 5275 • € • Vaporetto: San Samuele • gondolavenezia.it

Ca' Macana

2 Venice's mask culture is associated with Carnevale (see pp. 126–127). Brightly colored papier-mâché masks are adorned with feathers, beads, and baubles to help disguise the wearer's identity. Ca' Macana, one of the city's oldest mask-makers, offers one- and two-hour workshops at its Dorsoduro factory.

Calle Cappeller 3215 (workshop, prebooking essential) or Calle de le Boteghe 3172 (showroom) • 041 520 3229 • €€€€€ • Vaporetto: Ca' Rezzonico • camacana.com

Each visitor gets to make two masks at the Ca' Macana workshop.

Pasticceria Tonolo

3 Among the many specialties here are a sugar-dusted chocolate cake called *torta greca*, almond and sugar focaccia, as well as cookies, cream puffs, cannoli, and more. During Carnevale, you'll also find *frittelle* (Italian donuts).

Calle San Pantalon 3764 • 041 523 7209 • € • Vaporetto: San Tomà

Scuola Grande di San Rocco

4 Renaissance Venice reaches spectacular heights on the ceilings here and Tintoretto's late 16th-century paintings. Handheld mirrors help visitors view the lofty masterpieces.

Campo San Rocco • 041 523 4864 • €€€ (includes free audio guide) • Closed Jan. 1, Dec. 25 • Vaporetto: San Tomà • scuolagrandesanrocco.org

Gelateria White

5 Kids can create their own concoctions at this ice-cream parlor in the Rialto area. The self-service café features a dozen varieties of gelato and sorbet, plus an assortment of sauces and toppings to splash or sprinkle on top.

Ruga Vecchia San Giovanni 480 • 041 528 5109 • €€ • Vaporetto: Rialto Mercato

Mauro Vianello

6 For more than a thousand years, the city's glass factories have produced an incredible array of glass kitchenware, light fixtures, mirrors, and candlesticks. Master glassblower Mauro Vianello explains the process and creates delicate glass insects, sea animals, and musical instruments. Demonstrations take 30 minutes.

Artigianato d'Arte, Calle dei Morti 2251 • 041 520 1802 • €€ (prebooking essential) • Vaporetto: Rialto Mercato

GOOD **EATS**

■ AL VAPORETTO
A large selection of pasta, pizza, salads, and meat dishes make this trattoria near Campo Manin a great family choice. **Calle della Mandola 3726, 041 522 9498, €€**

■ ANTICO FORNO
Handcrafted pizzas and sandwiches are the forte of this takeout spot near the Rialto Market. **Ruga Vecchia San Giovanni 970, 041 520 4110, €**

■ LA ZUCCA
Introduce your kids to nouvelle Italian cuisine at this tucked-away café not far from Piazzale Roma. **Calle dello Spezier, 041 524 1570, €€**

Venice in a Weekend With Kids

Views from the sky and water, dinosaur bones, and a Disney-like stage show are among the highlights of this tour.

4 VizioVirtù Cioccolateria (see p. 48) Take the factory tour and munch miniature animals made from chocolate at this gourmet candy maker. Follow Calles Fava and Sant'Antonio west to Rialto "C" and board a vaporetto (line 1, N, or A) bound for San Stae. Walk south on Salizada San Stae, west on Calle del Tintor, and north on Salita Fontego.

5 Fondaco dei Turchi (see p. 49) Tucked inside the 13th-century Fondaco dei Turchi, Venice's excellent natural history collection offers plenty of hands-on fun. Retrace your steps (and vaporetto ride) to Rialto "C" and head east on the waterfront. Walk south on Per San Marco and west on Calle San Gallo beside the Teatro San Gallo.

6 Venezia the Show (see p. 49) This multimedia stage show about Venice combines comedy and education with live action and video projections.

Map labels:

CANNAREGIO
San Marcuola Casinò
Canal Grande
Riva de Biasio
Fondaco dei Turchi **5**
STRADA NOVA
San Stae
Ca' d'Oro
Rio Marin
CAMPO SAN GIACOMO DALL'ORIO
CAMPO BECCARIE
Rialto Mercato
CAMPO SANTA STIN
SAN POLO
Santa Maria Gloriosa dei Frari
Rio di San Polo
CAMPO SAN POLO
San Polo
San Silvestro
CAMPO DEI FRARI
Rio di San Polo
Canal Grande
Sant'Angelo
CAMPO SAN LUCA
CAMPO MANIN
Rio di Ca' Fascari
San Tomà
CAMPO SANTA MARGHERITA
CAMPO SANT' ANGELO
SAN MARCO
Teatro La Fenice
San Samuele
CAMPO SAN SAMUELE
CAMPO SANTO STEFANO
CAMPO SAN BARNABA
Ca' Rezzonico
CAMPO SAN MAURIZIO
DORSODURO
Accademia
PONTE DELL' ACCADEMIA
Santa Maria del Giglio
Salute
Rio di San Trovaso
Gallerie dell' Accademia
Collezione Peggy Guggenheim
Zattere
FONDAMENTA DELLE ZATTERE
Spirito Santo

VENICE WITH KIDS, DAY 2   DISTANCE: APPROX. 3 MILES (5 KM)
TIME: APPROX. 8–9 HOURS   START: SAN GIORGIO MAGGIORE

3 **Libreria Acqua Alta** (see p. 48)
Kids will love this crazy bookshop.
Retrace your steps to Campo Santa
Maria Formosa and meander northeast
on Calles Borgolocco, Marcello, and
Frutarol to the chocolate factory.

2 **Palazzo Querini Stampalia** (see p. 48)
Paintings of festivals, sports, carnival balls, and
other everyday events highlight the art and
artifacts inside this old palace. Cross the bridge
and follow the narrow lane northeast to Campo
Santa Maria Formosa and Calle Longa Santa
Maria Formosa, which leads to the bookshop.

Sacca
della
Misericordia

Canale della
Misericordia

REGIO

CAMPO DEI
SANTI
APOSTOLI

Ospedale

Rio dei Mendicanti

**VizioVirtù
Cioccolateria**
4

CAMPO
SANTI
GIOVANNI
E PAOLO

PONTE DI
RIALTO
Rialto

CAMPO
SANTA MARIA
FORMOSA

**Libreria
Acqua Alta**
3

CAMPO SAN
LORENZO

**Palazzo
Querini
Stampalla**
2

CASTELLO

Rio della Pietà

**Venezia
the Show**
6

Basilica di
San Marco

Bacino
Orseolo

PIAZZA
SAN
MARCO
Campanile di
San Marco

Palazzo
Ducale

PIAZZETTA
SAN
MARCO

RIVA DEGLI SCHIAVONI

San Zaccaria

**GIARDINI
EX REALI**
San Marco

*Bacino di
San Marco*

Punta della
Dogana

Canale di San Marco

ISOLA DI
SAN GIORGIO
MAGGIORE

San Giorgio

**Campanile di
San Giorgio
Maggiore**
1

0		400 meters
0		400 yards

1 **Campanile di San Giorgio Maggiore**
(see pp. 48, 90) Catch a vaporetto (line 2) to
San Giorgio Maggiore island and look down
on Venice from the top of the celebrated bell
tower. Hop on the ferry to San Zaccaria and
walk north on Calle de le Rasse. Continue
north to reach Calle dei Mercanti.

GOOD **EATS**

■ **HAPPY PIZZA**
This no-frills pizza parlor also serves pasta, wraps, calzone, and bruschetta at reasonable prices. **Calle dei Fabbri 828, €**

■ **HARD ROCK CAFÉ VENICE**
Burgers and steaks await at this canalside branch of the global chain. **Fondamenta Orseolo 1192 , 041 522 9665, €€**

■ **TAVERNA SAN LIO**
Simple pasta dishes for kids and seafood raviolis and anise-scented turbot for adults make this modest eatery a good lunch or dinner choice. **Salizada San Lio 5547–46, 041 277 0669, €€**

Campanile di San Giorgio Maggiore

1 Ride the elevator to the summit of the campanile beside the **Basilica di San Giorgio Maggiore** (see p. 90) for a sweeping panorama of the waterways and skyline. The wooden angel statue beside the ticket office was perched atop the tower until 1993, when it was struck by lightning.

Isola di San Giorgio Maggiore • 041 522 7827 • €
• Vaporetto: San Giorgio

Palazzo Querini Stampalia

2 Check out Gabriele Bella's "Scenes of Public Life in Venice," a series that includes a ball game, winter high jinx on a frozen canal, and a stick fight between two rival families on the Ponte Santa Fosca. Equally amusing are Pietro Longhi's scenes of gambling dens and masked balls.

Campo Santa Maria Formosa 5252 • 041 271 1411 • Closed Mon. • €€€
• Vaporetto: San Zaccaria, Rialto • querinistampalia.org

Libreria Acqua Alta

3 This rabbit warren of used books leads to a courtyard with a staircase made of waterlogged books. Snag some comics and see if the owners' cats are snoozing on the counters.

Calle Longa Santa Maria Formosa 5176/B • 041 296 0841 • Vaporetto: Ospedale, Rialto "C"

VizioVirtù Cioccolateria

4 Reenergize with some goodies from this gourmet chocolate maker, located in the same area where cocoa powder and spices were traded in the Middle Ages. Prebook an hour-long tasting tour.

Calle Forneri 5988 • 041 275 0149 • Closed Mon. • Vaporetto: Rialto "C"
• viziovirtu.com

Fondaco dei Turchi

5 Kids love this modern, interactive Natural History Museum. Exhibits range from dinosaur bones and whale skeletons to curiosities collected in Africa by Venetian explorers. **Tegnùe Aquarium** is also part of the collection.

Salita Fontego • 041 275 0206 • €€ • Closed Mon., Jan. 1, Dec. 25 • Vaporetto: San Stae • msn.visitmuve.it

Venezia the Show

6 Enjoy this lively, family-friendly journey through 1,500 years of Venetian history. The high-tech performance blends comedy and education with live stage actors and video projections. Performances are in English.

Campo San Gallo 1097 • 041 241 2002 • €€€€–€€€€€ (free for children age 9 and younger) • Vaporetto: San Marco, Rialto • teatrosangallo.net

The Natural History Museum is housed in this Veneto-Byzantine canalside palazzo.

PART 2

Venice's Neighborhoods

Venice's Neighborhoods

CANNAREGIO

Canale dello Misericordia

I Gesuiti
(Santa Maria
Assunta)

Rio dei Gesuiti

Fondamente Nove

FONDAMENTE NOVE

The Islands **150**

Rio dei Mendicanti

Ca'
d'Oro

Ca' d'Oro

Ospedale

Pescheria
CAMPO DELLA
PESCHERIA
Mercato   Rialto
di Rialto Mercato
Drogheria
Mascari
CAMPO SAN
GIACOMO DI RIALTO

CAMPO DEI
SANTI
APOSTOLI

San
Giovanni
Crisostomo

CORTE
SECONDA
DEL MILION

Santa Maria
del Miracoli

Monumento a
Bartolomeo
Colleoni

VizioVirtù

Scuola Grande
di San Marco

Santi Giovanni e Paolo
(San Zanipolo)

CAMPO
SANTI
GIOVANNI
E PAOLO

Chiesa di
Santa Maria
dei Derelitti

Rio di Santa Giustina

Celestia

CAMPO
DELLA
CONFRATERNITA

Caffè   PONTE DI
del Doge RIALTO

Rialto

Fondaco
dei Tedeschi

Cioccolateria

CAMPO
SANTA MARIA
FORMOSA

Acqua Alta

Castello 74

Chiesa di Santa
Maria Formosa

Palazzo
Grimani

Scuola Grande
di San Teodoro

Ca' Loredan

CAMPO
SAN LUCA

CAMPO
MANIN

SAN
MARCO

San Marco 54

CAMPO
SAN GALLO

Palazzo
Querini
Stampalia

Basilica di
San Marco

CAMPO
SAN
ZACCARIA

C A S T E L L O

Istituto
Ellenico

Chiesa di
San Zaccaria

Scuola di San Giorgio
degli Schiavoni

Rio della Pietà

CAMPO
BANDIERA
E MORO

Arsenale

San Giovanni
in Bragora

Museo
Correr

Harry's Bar

Bacino
Orseolo

PIAZZA
SAN
MARCO

Palazzo
Ducale

PIAZZETTA
SAN
MARCO

Campanile di
San Marco

GIARDINI
EX REALI

San Marco

Ponte
dei Sospiri

La Pietà

RIVA DEGLI SCHIAVONI

San Zaccaria

Hotel
Metropole

Arsenale

Museo
Storico
Navale

Salute

Bacino di
San Marco

Dogana
di Mare

Punta della
Dogana

Canale di San Marco

Santa
Maria
della
Salute

San Giorgio

San Giorgio Maggiore

ISOLA DI
SAN GIORGIO
MAGGIORE

Giardini della
Biennale
Internazionale
d'Arte

SAN MARCO

San Marco

San Marco is the most important of the city's six *sestieri* (neighborhoods). At its heart, Piazza San Marco (St. Mark's Square) epitomizes Venetian grandeur with its gondolas, Gothic Palazzo Ducale (Doge's Palace), and exotic, mosaic-laden Basilica di San Marco (St. Mark's Basilica). Nothing rivals the charm of this square in the morning as the cafés wake up to a new day. Beat the crowds to the major sights and then seek the more tranquil backwaters beyond. Almost completely surrounded by the Grand Canal, this *sestiere* has a wealth of canalside palaces, several of which are now galleries and museums. The neighborhood is also home to the Teatro La Fenice opera house—a landmark in the history of Italian theater. For destination shopping head to the Fondaco dei Tedeschi (Tedeschi Foundation) to the north of the neighborhood. Right beside the Ponte di Rialto (Rialto Bridge), this historic trading center houses four floors of luxury brands, an haute parfumerie, and locally sourced delicacies.

SAN MARCO

◀ **Piazza San Marco: The district revolves around this main square, in which the lively cafés and bars are always busy.**

San Marco

*East meets West on this grand tour centered on
Piazza San Marco, a showcase of power and glory.*

**❻ Teatro La
Fenice** (see
pp. 61–62) **Join**
a tour of this jewel
box of an opera
house, before
heading west via
Campo Sant'Angelo,
Campo Santo
Stefano, and Calle
Fruttarol to Campo
San Samuele.

❼ Palazzo Grassi (see p. 62) Visit this
powerhouse of contemporary art,
then relax on a short vaporetto
ride along the Grand Canal
from San Samuele to
Rialto, San Marco side.

SAN MARCO **DISTANCE: APPROX. 1.6 MILES (2.5 KM)**
TIME: APPROX. 7–8 HOURS **START: PIAZZA SAN MARCO**

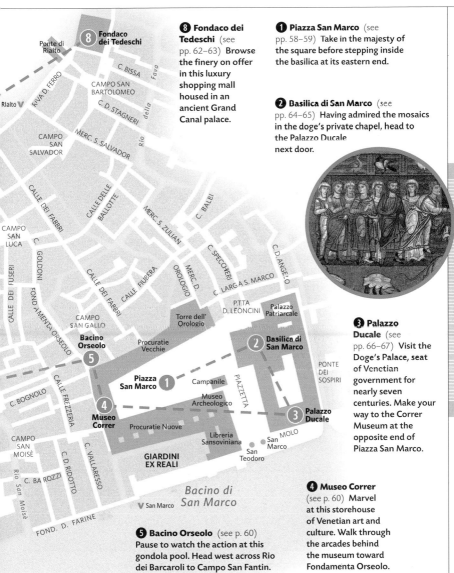

8 Fondaco dei Tedeschi (see pp. 62–63) Browse the finery on offer in this luxury shopping mall housed in an ancient Grand Canal palace.

1 Piazza San Marco (see pp. 58–59) Take in the majesty of the square before stepping inside the basilica at its eastern end.

2 Basilica di San Marco (see pp. 64–65) Having admired the mosaics in the doge's private chapel, head to the Palazzo Ducale next door.

3 Palazzo Ducale (see pp. 66–67) Visit the Doge's Palace, seat of Venetian government for nearly seven centuries. Make your way to the Correr Museum at the opposite end of Piazza San Marco.

4 Museo Correr (see p. 60) Marvel at this storehouse of Venetian art and culture. Walk through the arcades behind the museum toward Fondamenta Orseolo.

5 Bacino Orseolo (see p. 60) Pause to watch the action at this gondola pool. Head west across Rio dei Barcaroli to Campo San Fantin.

Map labels:

Ponte di Rialto
Rialto
RIVA D. FERRO
C. BISSA
Fava
CAMPO SAN BARTOLOMEO
C. D. STAGNERI
della
CAMPO SAN SALVADOR
MERC. S. SALVADOR
Rio
CALLE DEI FABBRI
CALLE DELLE BALLOTTE
MERC. S. ZULIAN
C. BALBI
CAMPO SAN LUCA
CALLE GOLDONI
CALLE DEI FABBRI
CALLE FIUBERA
MERC. D. OROLOGIO
C. SPECCHIERI
C. LARGA S. MARCO
C.D. ANGELO
CALLE DEI FUSERI
FOND. AMENT. ORSEOLO
CAMPO SAN GALLO
Torre dell' Orologio
P.TTA D. LEONCINI
Palazzo Patriarcale
Bacino Orseolo
Procuratie Vecchie
Piazza San Marco
Campanile
Basilica di San Marco
PONTE DEI SOSPIRI
C. BOGNOLO
CALLE FREZZERIA
Museo Correr
Procuratie Nuove
Museo Archeologico
PIAZZETTA
Palazzo Ducale
CAMPO SAN MOISE
C.D. RIDOTTO
C. VALLARESSO
Libreria Sansoviniana
San Teodoro
San Marco
MOLO
GIARDINI EX REALI
Rio San Moise
C. BA ROZZI
FOND. D. FARINE
San Marco
Bacino di San Marco

SAN MARCO

Piazza San Marco

1 The only true square in Venice, St. Mark's Square is both the ceremonial heart of the city and the center of modern Venetian life. A tantalizing blend of East and West, the square feels neither fully European nor Italian—an exotic legacy that lives on in its Byzantine domes, East Asian mosaics, and Gothic palaces. At one time the seat of government headed by the doge, ruler of the Venetian empire for many centuries, the square has also served as a prison and execution site, and a popular marketplace.

Flanking the eastern end of the piazza are the exuberantly decorated **Basilica di San Marco** (see pp. 64–65)—once the doge's private chapel—and the **Palazzo Ducale** (see pp. 66–67), the fairy-tale Doge's Palace, which borders the waterfront. The quayside here, known as **Bacino di San Marco,** is home to a busy gondola stand, where foreign dignitaries and ambassadors once moored their boats

The Piazzetta San Marco, with the Doge's Palace (left) and St. Mark's Library (right)

as they entered Venice. Opposite the basilica, at the western end of the piazza, is the **Museo Correr** (see p. 60), a dazzling introduction to Venetian art, history, and culture. On the northern flank of the square stands the Renaissance **Torre dell'Orologio** (Clock Tower; *041 271 5911, closed Jan. 1, Dec. 25, €€€—advance booking, torreorologio.visitmuve.it*). Look up to see its large astronomical clock face and, right at the top, two bell-striking Moors.

Piazza San Marco has no shortage of bars and cafés from which to watch the world go by, including **Caffè Florian** (*No. 57, 041 520 5641, €€, caffeflorian.com*), reputedly the oldest café in the world. Allow time during your visit to ride the elevator to the top of the 324-foot-tall (98.6 m) **Campanile** (St. Mark's Bell Tower; *041 270 8311, €€, basilicasanmarco .it*) for an impressive 360-degree view over the city. The tower is known locally as *el parón de casa*, the master of the house. During the republic, each of the tower's five bells played a different role — one summoning senators to the Doge's Palace, another (the execution bell) sounding the death knell. Today, the bells ring on the hour.

Piazza San Marco • Vaporetto: San Marco

IN **THE KNOW**

Piazza San Marco, dubbed the most famous drawing room in Europe by Napoleon Bonaparte, is framed by two granite columns at the lagoon end of the square, the Piazzetta. One 12th-century column is crowned by a winged lion, the symbol of Venice, representing St. Mark, while the other celebrates St. Theodore, the original patron saint. Venetians believe it is bad luck to walk between the columns, as this was once an execution site.

SAN MARCO

Basilica di San Marco

2 (see pp. 64–65)

Piazza San Marco • 041 270 8311 • Entry to the basilica is free; Museo €€; Tesoro €; Pala d'Oro € • Vaporetto: San Marco • basilicasanmarco.it

Palazzo Ducale

3 (see pp. 66–67)

Piazzetta San Marco 52 • 041 271 5911 • €€€€ • Vaporetto: San Marco • palazzoducale.visitmuve.it

Museo Correr

4 The Correr Museum houses several eclectic collections showcasing Venetian history. The **Neoclassical Rooms** and the **Imperial Rooms** on the ground floor are highlights. These rooms once served as the apartments of Napoleon and his Habsburg successors on visits to the city. An Empire-style ballroom sweeps into Habsburg Empress Sisi's brocaded suite, boudoir, and dining rooms. Pause in the **Throne Room** to admire Antonio Canova's coolly classical sculptures, from star-crossed lovers to mythical heroes. Entry to the museum also includes access to the **Biblioteca Nazionale Marciana** (St. Mark's Library; *041 240 7241, closed Jan. 1, Dec. 25*), the museum's crowning glory. Designed by Jacopo Sansovino in 1537, this authentic library is decorated by Tintoretto, Titian, and Veronese, the great artists of the day.

Piazza San Marco 52 • 041 4273 0892 • Closed Jan. 1, Dec. 25 • €€€€ • Vaporetto: San Marco • correr.visitmuve.it

GOOD **EATS**

■ **CANOVA**
Smooth service matched by classic Venetian and Italian cuisine ranging from lobster salad to scampi to sea bass. **Luna Baglioni, Calle Larga de l'Ascension, 041 528 9840, €€€**

■ **ENOTECA AL VOLTO**
Tuck in to Venetian tapas in a cozy, old-world inn off Campo San Luca, with local wines and light bites, from bruschetta and cheese to seafood spaghetti. **Calle Cavalli, 041 522 8945, €**

■ **LE MASCHERE**
An intimate courtyard restaurant with generous plates of lagoon spider crab, Parmesan risotto, and apple strudel—a legacy of the Austrian occupation. **Splendid Venice Hotel, San Marco Mercerie 760, 041 520 0755, €€**

Bacino Orseolo

5 To clear your head after a surfeit of art and culture, stop by the city's main gondola pool. You'll glimpse gondoliers chatting on bridges and making deals with travelers. You might also see the occasional delivery boat overladen with pumpkins and artichokes. This is the spot to watch a procession of gondolas drifting by, and also one of several places to book your own gondola adventure (see p. 175). If you are tempted, beware of paying more than the official rate and agree the route before setting off. For romance, stick to the back canals; for drama opt for the Grand Canal.

Calle del Salvadego • Vaporetto: San Marco

Teatro La Fenice

6 Even without a performance, there is enough splendor and scandal to enthrall you at the Venice Opera House. Christened "the Phoenix" in Italian, this jinxed treasure has been razed to the ground three times, most recently in 1996, but has always risen from the ashes. Following the last blaze, divas worldwide bewailed the loss of "the most beautiful opera house in the world." The rebuilding of La Fenice "as it was, where it was" was completed in 2003. Squeezed by canals, this restrained neoclassical opera house reveals a red and gold rococo interior in a horseshoe-shaped design. A visit to La Fenice includes a 45-minute audio tour (available in English), which covers the history of the theater, from the reborn auditorium to the gaudy royal box. You'll hear tales of Rossini and Bellini staging operas in this richly decorated auditorium, where glittering chandeliers compete with gilded balconies and

Gondolas jostle for space in the busy Bacino Orseolo.

SAVVY **TRAVELER**

Opera season at **La Fenice** runs
Jan.–July and Sept.–Oct., and
tickets at this 900-seat venue sell
out fast. Opera fans should avoid
disappointment by booking in
advance online (€€€€). The
theater also runs an impressive
schedule of symphonies
throughout the summer months.

stuccowork adorned with plump cherubs.
There is also a permanent exhibition devoted to
Maria Callas. If you're lucky, your visit to the
theater will coincide with a rehearsal. If not,
check the theater's event program and splash
out on an operatic performance. Choose the
front stalls rather than a box and join Venetian
high society in testing the power of the high Cs.

Campo San Fantin 1965 • 041 786 511 • €€€ • Vaporetto:
San Marco • teatrolafenice.it

Palazzo Grassi

7 The Grassi Palace is a slick showcase for rotating exhibitions
from the collections of proprietor François-Henri Pinault—
owner of Gucci, Château-Latour, and Christie's auction house.
Enlisting the services of Japanese architect Tadao Ando, Pinault has
turned this 18th-century palace on the Grand Canal into a hub of
contemporary art. Ando's minimalist exhibition spaces play against
the original neoclassical interior to spectacular effect. Tickets are
valid for 72 hours and include entry to an equally impressive sister
venue in Dorsoduro, the **Punta della Dogana** (Museum of
Contemporary Art; see p. 137), although both venues are open
only when holding exhibitions. Recent shows at the Palazzo Grassi
include a collection of 130 previously unseen photographs by
Irving Penn. Whatever the exhibition in progress during your visit,
be sure to look out for challenging canalside installations, too.

Campo San Samuele 3231 • 041 271 9031 • Closed Tues. • €€€ • Vaporetto: San
Samuele • palazzograssi.it

Fondaco dei Tedeschi

8 The 800-year-old Tedeschi Foundation (also *fontego* in the
Venetian dialect), named for the historic headquarters of the
German merchants, was once the most important trading center in
the Rialto area. Today, following extensive remodeling by the Dutch

The understated exterior of the Tedeschi Foundation

architect Rem Koolhaas, the building is now a four-story luxury goods megastore. This severe-looking emporium was built in 1228 and remains the city's second largest building. Originally, it served as a mercantile hub and, for centuries, was used to trade spices, silks, and exotic goods between the Far East and Europe. Now, alongside the latest trends in men's and women's fashion you'll find an haute parfumerie and a high-end shoe salon. The building also houses new arts and exhibition spaces and has a rooftop terrace. If you are looking for special Italian gifts to take home and other local products, you need venture no farther than the first floor. When you've finished shopping, don't miss the opportunity to admire the distinctive **Ponte di Rialto** (Rialto Bridge; see p. 114) linking the neighborhoods of noble San Marco and mercantile San Polo.

Salizada Fontego dei Tedeschi • Vaporetto: San Marco

Basilica di San Marco

Modeled on the churches of Constantinople, this exotic basilica transposes the essence of Byzantine splendor to the West.

The facade of the basilica features the winged lion that has come to symbolize Venice.

The basilica was consecrated in A.D. 832 as a mausoleum for St. Mark's relics and as the doge's ceremonial chapel. In 976, the church burned down but was rebuilt between 1063 and 1094, its layout based on the Greek cross. The result is an eclectic yet harmonious design, with an ornate stonework facade and five onion-bulb domes. Inside, the building is remarkable for its spatial complexity and stylistic fusion, its mosaics being one of the chief glories. Visitors are channeled along set routes, making lingering difficult.

Shimmering Mosaics

Stepping inside the basilica is akin to entering a mosque or a sultan's palace. The interior is studded with mosaics, many of them glistening with gold leaf. Even the windows of this extravaganza were walled up to make space for more mosaics. They depict biblical scenes, including, in the **Pentecost dome** above the nave, the descent of the Holy Spirit as a dove. The *pavimento* (basilica floor) mosaics resemble an oriental carpet, interweaving floral, animal, and geometric motifs.

The Altar and Pala d'Oro

St. Mark's remains (see p. 68) are supposedly encased under **the altar,** although skeptics believe that these were destroyed in the fire of A.D. 976. Behind the altar, often swamped by crowds, is the **Pala d'Oro,** a medieval altarpiece studded with gems, made by craftsmen from Constantinople but embellished by the Venetians.

The Treasury

After the conquest of Constantinople in 1204, Venice celebrated its triumph with the display of Byzantine booty.

IN THE KNOW

A few steps from the **Pala d'Oro,** look for a heart-shaped stone cut into the floor. This marks the burial place of the heart of Doge Francesco Erizzo (d. 1646), who requested that his heart be buried here (his body is buried at his place of birth). Two more shapes are cut within the heart: a doge's cap and a hedgehog—Erizzo's family emblem.

The **Tesoro** (Treasury), dating from the ninth-century **Palazzo Ducale** (see pp. 66–67), displays a wealth of Byzantine gold, silver, and glassware.

The Museum

Above the entrance portal to the basilica, you'll find the **Museo di San Marco** (St. Mark's Museum), currently home to the bronze classical horses that once graced the Hippodrome in Constantinople. You'll have seen copies of the horses—nostalgic symbols of Venetian independence—above the main portal before entering the basilica. Before leaving, stand on the upstairs **loggia** to enjoy sweeping views of Piazza San Marco.

Piazza San Marco • 041 270 8311 • Entry to the Basilica is free; Museo €€; Tesoro €; Pala d'Oro €
• Vaporetto: San Marco • basilicasanmarco.it

SAN MARCO

Palazzo Ducale

Pad through this high Gothic, frescoed palace to imagine life as the supreme ruler of the Serene Republic of Venice.

The Sala del Maggior Consiglio features Domenico and Jacopo Tintoretto's "Paradise."

From the ninth century to the fall of the republic in 1797, the Palazzo Ducale was the powerhouse of Venice. This Doge's Palace was also the seat of Venetian government and encompassed the city's grand law courts and grim state prisons. The doge was a "glorified slave of the Republic" who lived in a gilded cage and was closely guarded in the "shadow-palace" that also concealed a police state backed by steely inquisitors, secret passageways, and a mail drop for sneaky denunciations.

■ COLONNADED COURTYARD

As you enter the palace courtyard, look up to the columns of the first-floor gallery—two pink ones mark the spot from where death sentences were announced. The courtyard's triumphal **Scala dei Giganti** (Giants' Stairway) is lavishly sculpted with figures of Mars and Neptune, symbolizing Venetian supremacy on land and sea. Doges were once crowned with a ceremonial jewel-encrusted cap at the top of these stairs.

■ STATE APARTMENTS

Climb the monumental **Scala dei Censori** (Stairs of the Censors) to the doge's apartments on the first floor. Here, the walls of the **Sala dello Scudo** (Shield Room) are lined with maps of the empire in its heyday. A terrace allowed the doge private access to the **Basilica di San Marco** (see pp. 64–65), and a secret staircase leads to the floor above (accessed as part of the **Secret Itinerary** tour).

■ CEREMONIAL ROOMS

At the top of the **Scala d'Oro** (Golden Staircase) on the second floor, you are greeted by a **Bocca della Verità,** a

SAVVY **TRAVELER**

For a touch of the macabre, explore the state inquisitors' rooms, torture chamber, and prisons on the **Secret Itinerary** tour *(041 4273 0892, €€€€€, vivaticket.it),* accessed at the top of the Scala D'Oro. Tours are given daily, in English, at 9:55 a.m., 10:55 a.m., and 11:35 a.m. Advance booking essential.

gaping "mouth of truth" mail drop into which citizens posted secret denunciations. The ceremonial rooms beyond offer a glorious showcase of Venetian art, sculpture, and craftsmanship. In the **Sala del Maggior Consiglio** (Grand Council Chamber) is the doge's throne. This vast room is studded with paintings that include Veronese's **"Apotheosis of Venice."**

■ PRISON LIFE

The **Prigioni** (prisons) confirm the shadowy side of the palace, a secretive machine staffed by state inquisitors, spies, and torturers-in-residence. Shuffle over the **Ponte dei Sospiri** (Bridge of Sighs), named after the sadness felt by the newly convicted, glimpsing their beloved lagoon for the last time.

SAN MARCO

Piazzetta San Marco 52 • 041 271 5911 • €€€€ • Vaporetto: San Marco • palazzoducale.visitmuve.it

La Serenissima

At the height of its power and prosperity, the Most Serene Republic of Venice —La Serenissima—was viewed by its contemporaries with a mixture of both envy and amazement. How could this city built by refugees on little more than water and mud have grown into a trading center of fabled wealth and the ruler of a far-flung Mediterranean empire?

A Byzantine chalice from the treasury in the Basilica di San Marco
Opposite: Canaletto's "The Betrothal of the Venetian Doge to the Adriatic Sea,"
ca. 1729–30

Humble Beginnings

In the dark and dangerous centuries that followed the fall of the Roman Empire in western Europe, people fleeing the insecurity of the war-ravaged Italian mainland established scattered settlements on the mudflats of the tidal lagoon. Venice—then known as Rivoalto, and later Rialto—was one settlement among others, no more substantial than Torcello, Murano, or Burano. Then, in 829, two Venetian merchants stole the corpse of St. Mark the Evangelist from Muslim-ruled Alexandria and smuggled it to Rivoalto in a pork barrel. The **Basilica di San Marco** (see pp. 64–65) was built to house this holy relic and, expanding around the basilica, the city of Venice began its rise to fame.

The technical feat involved in building Venice was one of its chief wonders. Dozens of small mud banks, intersected by channels of water, had to be transformed into a city of brick and stone. Builders drove wooden piles into plots of earth drained of water in order to build their impressive three- or four-story buildings.

Protected by water from possible enemies from the land, the city devoted its resources to becoming a major power at sea. By 1000, Venice was the dominant force in the Adriatic, its ships carrying Crusader knights to Palestine (at a price) and its merchants making fortunes importing luxury goods from the East to northwest Europe. A string of colonies on Mediterranean coasts provided bases for the Venetian naval and commercial fleets.

Mercantile Rule

Being merchants, not landowners, the Venetians ran their city more like a business than a traditional territorial state. Rejecting the hereditary principle in government that was common throughout Europe at the time, the wealthiest families elected one of their own number to lead Venice as "doge." The doge was elected for life, but was not allowed to give any member of his own family a position of power or to have any say in the choice of his successor. Voting was

limited to heads of high-status families listed in the Golden Book, a tome kept under lock and key in the Doge's Palace. Numbering some 1,200 men, these nobles formed the city's Grand Council.

The city's wealth and power peaked in the 15th century. Venice spread its rule over a large area of northern Italy, but this expansion sucked the city into the destructive wars that engulfed Italian states in the Renaissance period. Worse still, it encountered an enemy in the eastern Mediterranean whose power and resources it could not match: the Turkish Ottoman Empire. The fall of Christian Constantinople to the Muslim Ottomans in 1453 was a disaster for Venice. Its privileged position in the eastern Mediterranean was lost. The Ottomans built a powerful fleet and began mopping up Venetian colonies. Despite victories that included the Battle of Lepanto in 1571, the undoing of the Venetian seaborne empire was slow, taking two centuries, but the decline was irreversible.

The Holy League in battle with the Ottomans at Lepanto, October 1571 (Antonio Vassilacchi, 1600)

Palazzo Grassi, the last palace built on the Grand Canal

The Venetian elite defended its power with the same ruthlessness it brought to the accumulation of wealth. From 1310 a secretive Council of Ten was entrusted with suppressing subversion and corruption within the Venetian Republic. It ran a system of police spies who fed suspects to the Ten's notorious prison cells and torture chambers. Those identified as enemies of the state might face public mutilation and execution, or be silently "disappeared" by drowning at night.

SAN MARCO

End of an Era

By the 18th century, Venice was regarded first and foremost as a city of pleasure, a delight for the curious foreign visitor in search of frivolous entertainment. No longer able to defend itself against a major power, the Most Serene Republic was allowed to survive until 1797, when French general and future emperor Napoleon Bonaparte ordered its dissolution in the name of the revolution, plundering the city of many of its treasures. Having lost control of its fate, Venice passed from the hands of the French to Austrian rule, before ending up as a provincial backwater in newly united Italy from 1866. The final collapse of the city has long been predicted, with declining population, worsening pollution, and the gradual sinking of the entire physical structure into the lagoon. But the glorious relics of the Serenissima have continued to survive against the odds, defying the prophets of doom.

Nightlife

Unlike other cities in Europe, Venice is not known for clubs and discos that run into the early hours. Instead, Venetians like to relax listening to classical music or jazz in one of several live music venues, linger over a spritz as they watch the sun go down, or live it up a little in one of the city's many campos.

■ MUSIC VENUES

Historically, an evenings' entertainment would have been in the form of a concert. In San Marco, the **Scuola Grande di San Teodoro** *(San Marco 4810, 041 528 7227, €€€, scuolagrandesanteodoro.it)*, near Rialto, hosts evenings of opera or Vivaldi's *Four Seasons* in which musicians and singers perform in full Venetian costume. In Dorsoduro, the **Scuola Grande San Giovanni di Evangelista** *(Campo San Vio, 345 791 1948, €€€, venicemusicproject.it)* offers concerts of classical music and opera from March through October. For live music, head to **Osteria all'Alba** *(Ramo del Fontego dei Tedeschi 380, 340 124 56 34, €)*, a great San Marco bar with bands playing every weekend. For live jazz, the **Venice Jazz Club** *(Dorsoduro 3102, 041 523 2056, €€€, Closed Thurs., Sun., venicejazzclub.com)*, has music every night from 9 p.m.

■ SUNSETS AND SPRITZ

A beautiful way to begin an evening is to do as the Venetians do, and catch the sunset while drinking a spritz. In Castello, **Bar Terrazza Danieli** *(Riva degli Schiavoni 4196, 041 522 6480, €€€€)*, the upmarket rooftop terrace bar of the prestigious Hotel Danieli looks directly out across the lagoon. On the Zattere in the Dorsoduro *sestiere*, the small waterfront kiosk bar **El Chioschetto** *(Fondamenta Zattere al Ponte Lungo 1406, 348 396 8466, €)* is the place to catch a magnificent view of the sun dipping behind the Venetian skyline. And, in Cannaregio, you can watch the sun sink into the Grand Canal at **Taverna del Campiello Remer** *(Cannaregio 5701, 041 522 8789, €€, alremer.it)*. Simply dangle your legs off the pier and soak up the last rays of the sun overlooking the **Mercato di Rialto** (Rialto Market; see pp. 114–115).

Alfresco tables beside the Rialto Bridge, San Marco

■ BARHOPPING THE VENETIAN WAY
The bar scene in Venice is different to that in many other cities, and is dominated by small bars where people stand outside, even in the winter time. In San Polo, there is always a buzz in the **Campo Cesare Battisti già della Bella Vienna,** near the Mercato di Rialto. Right beside the vaporetto stop, **Muro** (*San Polo 222, 041 241 2339, €, murovinoecucina.it),* with its sidewalk tables and loud music, is always packed with locals and travelers alike. **Al Mercà** (*Campo Bella Vienna 213, 346 834 0660, €)* is a tiny,

counter-based bar with a great wine list. Slip under the archways into Campo San Giacomo di Rialto to find **Banco Giro** (*San Polo 122, 041 523 2061, €).* Here, you can stand under the arches of the Tribunale di Venezia on one side or sit overlooking the Grand Canal on the other. Night owls should head to the area around **Campo Santa Margherita** (see p. 139) in Dorsoduro. **Café Noir** (*Dorsoduro 3805, 041 528 0956 €–€€),* has a lively atmosphere, and **Osteria alla Bifora** (*Dorsoduro 2930, 041 523 6119, €€),* a beautiful interior.

Castello

Perched at the eastern end of Venice, this neighborhood served as the city's hardworking underbelly during the Middle Ages and the Renaissance—the location of the hectic docks onto which goods from around the world were unloaded, and the sprawling shipyards that created and maintained Venice's maritime might. In modern times, Castello is the largest and most diverse of the city's six *sestieri*. The old wharves have morphed into pleasant waterfront promenades and the Arsenale naval complex has become one of the main venues for the prestigious Venice Biennale of art and architecture. Castello also flaunts bravura churches—notably La Pietà and Santi Giovanni e Paolo—several of the city's richly decorated *scuole grandi* (great schools), and museums that focus on maritime and medical history. With more land to spare—and more in the works via reclamation—the district also sports more parks and green spaces than the other districts, making it a great place to take a load off once in a while, and simply enjoy the view.

◄ **A couple wearing traditional clothes dance on the Riva degli Schiavoni, during Carnevale.**

Castello

*The city's east end offers waterside promenades,
eclectic architecture, and an impregnable maritime fortress.*

❶ Santi Giovanni e Paolo (see pp. 84–85) Admire Bellini's polyptych and the multilayered high altar in this massive basilica before stepping out into the campo that fronts the church.

❷ Scuola Grande di San Marco (see pp. 78–79) Across the square, visit this institution dedicated to St. Mark. Walk south to Campo Santa Maria Formosa and the church of the same name.

❸ Church of Santa Maria Formosa (see pp. 79–80) Seek out the grotesque stone face at this quirky church. Head south on Salita Corte Rotta through the Campo San Zaccaria to the waterfront.

❹ Riva degli Schiavoni (see p. 80) Grab lunch while you soak up the view across the water to San Giorgio. Head east on the quay past the equestrian statue.

❺ La Pietà (see pp. 80–81) Vivaldi was choirmaster at this 18th-century church, renowned for its fine acoustics. Cut down Calle de la Pietà beside the church and cross onto Fondamenta Furlani.

**CASTELLO DISTANCE: APPROX. 4.5 MILES (7.2 KM)
TIME: APPROX. 7-8 HOURS START: CAMPO SS. GIOVANNI E PAOLO**

CASTELLO

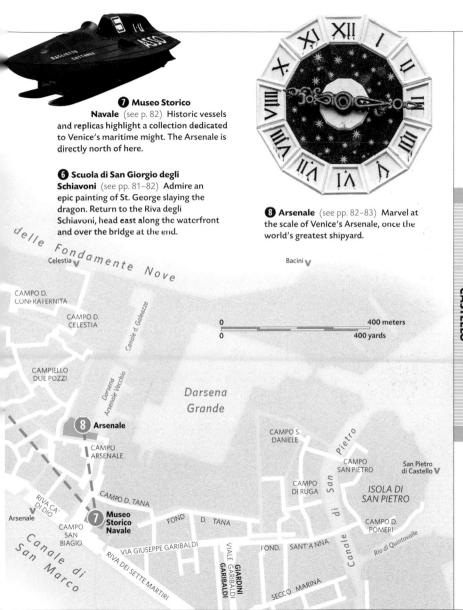

❼ Museo Storico Navale (see p. 82) Historic vessels and replicas highlight a collection dedicated to Venice's maritime might. The Arsenale is directly north of here.

❻ Scuola di San Giorgio degli Schiavoni (see pp. 81–82) Admire an epic painting of St. George slaying the dragon. Return to the Riva degli Schiavoni, head east along the waterfront and over the bridge at the end.

❽ Arsenale (see pp. 82–83) Marvel at the scale of Venice's Arsenale, once the world's greatest shipyard.

delle Fondamente Nove

Celestia ▾

Bacini ▾

CAMPO D. CONFRATERNITA

CAMPO D. CELESTIA

Canale d. Galeazze

0   400 meters
0   400 yards

CAMPIELLO DUE POZZI

Darsena Arsenale Vecchio

Darsena Grande

❽ Arsenale

CAMPO ARSENALE

CAMPO S. DANIELE

San Pietro

CAMPO SAN PIETRO

San Pietro di Castello ▾

CAMPO DI RUGA

ISOLA DI SAN PIETRO

RIVA CA' DI DIO

Arsenale

❼ Museo Storico Navale

CAMPO D. TANA

FOND. D. TANA

Canale di San

CAMPO D. POMERI

Rio di Quintavalle

CAMPO SAN BIAGIO

VIA GIUSEPPE GARIBALDI

FOND. SANT'ANNA

Canale di San Marco

RIVA DEI SETTE MARTIRI

VIALE GARIBALDI

GIARDINI GARIBALDI

SECCO MARINA

CASTELLO

Santi Giovanni e Paolo

1 (See pp. 84–85)

Campo dei Santi Giovanni e Paolo • 041 523 7510 • € • Vaporetto: Ospedale
• basilicasantigiovanniepaolo.it

Scuola Grande di San Marco

2 Sharing the square with **Santi Giovanni e Paolo** is a smaller, but much more elaborate structure dedicated to St. Mark. Contrary to the name, Venice's *scuole grandi* (great schools) were not educational institutions but rather religious charitable organizations, similar in form and function to the modern Knights of Columbus. San Marco was one of the grandest, a powerful and wealthy confraternity that cared for destitute Venetians, arranged religious processions, and avidly supported the arts. Their breathtaking headquarters were erected in the late 15th century,

The winged lion of St. Mark graces the ornate facade of the Scuola Grande di San Marco.

a masterful design by architect and sculptor Pietro Lombardo that flaunts both Renaissance and Byzantine influences. See how the white marble facade stands in stark contrast to the dour red brick of the adjacent basilica. For many years only the ground floor of the *scuola* was open to visitors, supported by 10 Corinthian columns and stripped of much of its original decoration. But in 2013, the school unveiled the wonderfully restored **Sala Capitolare** on the second floor. Although the room houses a very interesting collection of antique medical books and instruments, its main feature is an ornately carved 16th-century wooden ceiling by Vettor Scienza da Feltre and Lorenzo di Vincenzo da Trento, as well as paintings by various artists depicting scenes from the life of St. Mark.

Campo dei Santi Giovanni e Paolo • 041 529 4323 • Closed Mon., Sun. • € • Vaporetto: Ospedale • scuolagrandesanmarco.it

GOOD **EATS**

■ **ALLA RIVETTA**
Traditional lagoon platters are the forte of this backstreet trattoria near the Ponte San Provolo. Fritto misto and spaghetti with clams are staples. **Salizada San Provolo 4625, 041 528 7302, €€**

■ **OSTERIA OLIVA NERA**
Order the seafood carpaccio or fritto misto at this charming *osteria* that serves Venetian recipes with a modern twist. **Castello 3417/3447, 041 522 2170, €€€**

■ **TERRAZZA DANIELI**
This rooftop restaurant atop the Hotel Danieli dazzles with its views of the Bacino di San Marco and Venetian skyline. **Riva degli Schiavoni 4196, 041 522 6480, €€€€**

Church of Santa Maria Formosa

3 This quirky church on a busy market square boasts two facades, an unusual bell tower, and a cryptic stone face. Santa Maria Formosa was erected in the early 16th century on the remains of an earlier church that had burned to the ground. Architect Mauro Codussi decided to utilize the Greek cross floor plan of the previous chapel rather than stretch the design into a Latin cross. The shrine derives its odd name (meaning "buxom" in Italian) from a seventh-century Venetian bishop who claimed visions of a well-endowed Virgin Mary. Also atypical is the baroque bell tower with its geometric motifs and grotesque stone face called the *mascherone*—a bearded, buck-toothed figure strategically placed at the base of the tower to ward off mischievous bell-ringing demons. The interior of the church reverts to traditional religious motifs like "Madonna and Child with St. Dominic" by Giambattista Tiepolo, "The Last Supper" by Leandro Bassano, and Palma il Vecchio's St. Barbara polyptych.

Campo Santa Maria Formosa • 041 523 4645 • Closed Sun. • € • Vaporetto: Ospedale, Rialto, San Zaccaria • santamariaformosa.it

Riva degli Schiavoni

4 Stretching between **Piazza San Marco** (St. Mark's Square; see pp. 58–59) and the **Arsenale** (Arsenal; see pp. 82–83), this popular promenade is crowded with food and craft stalls, outdoor cafés, boat docks, and plenty of spots to snap photos of maritime action in the busy Bacino di San Marco. Named for the Slavic seamen who plied the Adriatic between Venice and the Dalmatian coast, the quay was once lined with Renaissance palaces, some of which were later converted into hotels. About halfway along is an equestrian statue of Victor Emmanuel II, modern Italy's first king.

Between Rio di Palazzo and Rio Ca' di Dio on the Bacino di San Marco • Vaporetto: Arsenale, San Marco, San Zaccaria

La Pietà

5 This 18th-century shrine is also called the Vivaldi Church because of its association with the famed composer. It was commissioned as the church for the Ospedale della Pietà, a combination convent, orphanage, and music school at which Antonio Vivaldi taught violin and served as choirmaster off and on between 1703 and 1740. He also composed instrumental and vocal music specifically for performances in the original La Pietà. Designed by Giorgio Massari, the current structure is a remodeling of that earlier chapel, and arose shortly after the composer's death in 1741. The oval shape imbues the interior with excellent acoustics that visitors can savor during the many concerts that are staged here throughout the year. Currently, they are performed by **I Virtuosi Italiani** (0366 403 9753, €€€€€, chiesavivaldi.it), orchestra in

CASTELLO

The "Visitation of Mary to St. Elizabeth" in La Pietà

residence since 2011. Among La Pietà's artworks are the ceiling fresco "Coronation of the Virgin" by Giambattista Tiepolo and above the altarpiece, "Visitation of Mary to St. Elizabeth" by Giambattista Piazzetta and Giuseppe Angeli.

Riva degli Schiavoni • 041 522 2171 • Closed Mon. • € • Vaporetto: San Zaccaria
• chiesavivaldi.it

Scuola di San Giorgio degli Schiavoni

6 Headquarters for another of the Catholic confraternities that flourished in medieval and Renaissance Venice, San Giorgio is tucked down a canal that runs off the Riva degli Schiavoni. As the name suggests, there is also a Slavic connection here—the Dalmatian expats who founded this great school dedicated their charitable institution to Sts. George, Jerome, and Tryphone and commissioned Vittore Carpaccio to render paintings of these three

IN **THE KNOW**

First staged in 1895, the **Biennale di Venezia** *(041 521 8711, labiennale.org)* is one of the globe's oldest and most ambitious artistic events. This "biennial" is actually held annually, but with the arts celebrated in odd years and architecture celebrated in even years. The result is an eclectic, chic, challenging, and commercially successful showcase of contemporary ideas. Revolving around the Arsenale complex in Castello, it takes place in structures that are often closed to the public.

patron saints to decorate the lower hall. Most striking of these is an epic image of St. George and the dragon that rather graphically includes the remains of the dragon's most recent victims.

Calle dei Furlani • 041 522 8828 • € • Vaporetto: Arsenale, San Zaccaria

Museo Storico Navale

7 Although it is run by the Italian Navy, the Maritime Museum is located outside the **Arsenale** (Arsenal) walls in a restored 15th-century granary overlooking the Bacino di San Marco. The collection covers the thousand-year span of Venice's maritime glory from the Middle Ages through World War II. Scattered throughout its 42 rooms are naval uniforms, ship models, nautical instruments, and shipyard tools, as well as a replica Venetian war galley and the *Scalé Reale* barge—the latter, once used by the city's doges. Art collector Peggy Guggenheim's over-the-top private gondola is also on show here.

Riva San Biasio 2148 • 041 244 1399 • €€ • Closed Sun. • Vaporetto: Arsenale, San Zaccaria • marina.difesa.it

Arsenale

8 Perched at the city's eastern extreme, this waterfront warren was once the world's largest shipyard and home to a fleet that provided the muscle behind Venice's domination of the eastern Mediterranean. In modern times, it has morphed into a multiuse compound that embraces the arts, science, and Italian Navy. Founded in the 12th century, the Arsenale mass-produced and provisioned as many as 3,000 warships for the Venetian Republic's merchant princes and mercenary sea captains. During its 16th-century apex, the shipyard employed 16,000 workers who could collectively produce a new war galley from start to finish

CASTELLO

The Arsenale's main gate, the Porta Magna, was built in around 1460.

every 24 hours. By the mid-20th century, much of the Arsenale was vacant and derelict. Its savior was a **Biennale di Venezia** (see opposite) request to use part of the old shipyard as a temporary gallery. Since then, many of the old workshops, warehouses, and dry docks have been refurbished into venues for various Biennale exhibits or permanent galleries and research labs. If you are fortunate to visit during the Biennale, you'll have access to various sites that are otherwise closed to the public. These include the **Artiglierie,** a former gun workshop, the **Corderia,** a workshop in which ships' ropes were once made, and the **Gaggiandre,** an arcaded dry dock with a design attributed to Jacopo Sansovino. The Napoleonic-era **Porta Nuova** guard tower has also been restored, as has the structure that now houses the **Arsenale Visitor Center**.

Sestiere Castello • 041 241 2020 • Closed Sat., Sun. • Vaporetto: Celestia, Bacini/ Arsenale Nord

Santi Giovanni e Paolo

A Gothic exterior safeguards the Renaissance and baroque treasures found inside this massive basilica near Venice's northern shore.

The interior of Santi Giovanni e Paolo, the last resting place of 25 Venetian doges

Venice's second most important church after the Basilica di San Marco (see pp. 64–65), the Basilica of Sts. John and Paul is affectionately known as San Zanipolo. Its Gothic facade is full of eye-catching details. The stone sarcophagi of various doges flank a central doorway by Bartolomeo Bon that includes a 13th-century Byzantine figure of the Virgin Mary and an archangel. The eye rises from there to the massive rose window and three white tabernacles perched along the roofline that shelter figures of Sts. Dominic, Peter, and Thomas Aquinas.

■ The Nave

A row of tombs flanks the lofty nave with its immense stone columns. Trying to outdo their predecessors even in death, the doges and their condottieri (mercenary generals) built ever more elaborate funerary monuments. Doge Nicolò Marcello reclines atop an elegant sarcophagus, Doge Andrea Vendramin beneath a Roman-style triumphal arch, while Captain-General Niccolò di Pitigliano rides a golden stallion. The right side of the nave also contains two baroque chapels and Giovanni Bellini's extraordinary St. Vincent Ferrer polyptych. On the opposite wall, a door integrated into the tomb of artist Palma the Younger opens into a sacristy filled with 16th- and 17th-century Dominican artworks.

■ The High Altar

A masterpiece of baroque artistry and craftsmanship, the soaring altar was created by Baldassare Longhena, a 17th-century Venetian architect. Light filtering through the stained-glass windows on either side—including an original 15th-century Murano creation

IN **THE KNOW**

One of Venice's most attractive squares, the **Campo Santi Giovanni e Paolo** has long been a favorite with artists. Canaletto was still in his 20s when he painted the scene here in 1724–26, a work that hangs in the **Ca' Rezzonico** museum (see p. 138). Also in the square, you'll see a monument dedicated to the mercenary general Bartolomeo Colleoni. It is the only equestrian monument to have been erected by the Venetian Republic.

in the south transept—illuminates various saints arrayed across the altar, among them, the two martyrs for whom the church is named.

■ Chapel of Our Lady of the Rosary

The basilica's crown jewel was created in 1582 to commemorate the Venetian victory over the Turkish fleet at Lepanto (see p. 70). Although masterpieces by Titian, Bellini, and Tintoretto were lost in an 1867 fire, the rebuilt chapel (1959) is lavishly decorated by three circular ceiling panels by Paolo Veronese, marble statues by Alessandro Vittoria, and works by other Renaissance artists.

CASTELLO

Campo Santi Giovanni e Paolo • 041 523 7510 • € • Vaporetto: Ospedale
• basilicasantigiovanniepaolo.it

Maritime City

The most solemn annual festival of the Most Serene Republic of Venice (A.D. 697–1797) was the "marriage of the sea" on Ascension Day, when the doge cast a consecrated ring into the ocean. The ceremony symbolized the unbreakable link between the city and the sea. At the time, Venice's prosperity and its very survival depended almost entirely upon its maritime trade and the strength of its naval forces.

A Venetian galley under sail
Opposite: A 16th-century oil painting depicting Venetian shipbuilders at work

Supremacy at Sea

The state-run shipyards of the **Arsenale** (Arsenal; see pp. 82–83), founded in 1200, were the largest industrial enterprise in Europe. The vessels manufactured there were mostly oared galleys, the characteristic ships of the Mediterranean since the time of ancient Greece. At its peak in the 1400s, Venice possessed 3,000 ships and almost 40,000 of the city's population were sailors of some kind.

Part of Venice's fortune was made by providing sea transport for armies of knights who, from the 11th to the 13th centuries, traveled to fight the Crusades against Muslims in Palestine and Syria. The city charged a hefty fee for carrying the men with all their horses and equipment. From around 1330, fleets of large merchant galleys sailed annually from Venice eastward to Crimea in the Black Sea, where they collected goods brought overland on the Silk Route from China, and westward out into the Atlantic, sailing to ports in Flanders and in England. Venetian naval power was essential in promoting trade. As well as protecting merchant fleets, its naval galleys fought vicious turf wars against trade rivals, such as the Genoese and the Pisans. Sea power enabled Venice to establish and sustain a series of colonial possessions around the eastern Mediterranean, the Adriatic, and the Aegean.

A Redundant Fleet

By the 16th century, sailing ships from Europe's Atlantic coast had begun opening up oceanic trade routes, leaving the Mediterranean as a relative backwater. The ships could carry far more cannon than a war galley, so the Venetian mode of naval warfare became outdated. The last great battle in which Venetian galleys fought was at Lepanto in 1571. After that, Venice's maritime empire and its status as a seafaring state went into terminal decline.

THE **GONDOLA**

In the 16th century, some 10,000 gondolas plied the Venetian canals, carrying both people and cargo. A city ordinance of 1562 ruled that they could be any color as long as it was black. The gondolas were built in small boatyards called *squeri,* one of which can still be seen in operation at San Trovaso, off the Zattere in the Dorsoduro neighborhood (see p. 89). Today, around 500 gondolas are still afloat, exclusively serving the tourist trade.

CASTELLO

Secret Backwaters

The elbow-to-elbow ambience common in Piazza San Marco and at the Ponte di Rialto is in marked contrast to the more obscure parts of Venice that remain far, far from the madding crowds. For those who cherish offbeat—and don't mind walking a little farther—these charming backwaters offer welcome relief.

■ EASTERN CASTELLO

Tiny islands float off Castello's eastern shore, each with its own treasures. **San Pietro di Castello** is where urban Venice first took root in the sixth century. The castle that gave the island its name is long gone, leaving the **Basilica di San Pietro di Castello** (*Campo San Pietro, 041 275 0462, €*) as the predominant landmark. This impressive Renaissance-style church served as the city's official Roman Catholic cathedral from 1451 to 1807. In addition to a campanile of white Istrian stone, San Pietro also features Pietro Liberi's epic "Plague of Serpents" and a legendary stone throne made from Arab stelae. Neighboring **Sant'Elena** island harbors the city's largest green space, the waterfront Parco delle Rimembranze with its shady lanes, playgrounds, and monuments to Verdi, Wagner, and those who fell in World War II.

■ SAN TROVASO

Centered around a church and canal of the same name, the San Trovaso neighborhood spans the Dorsoduro *sestiere* between the Grand Canal and the Giudecca Canal. Erected in the late 16th and early 17th centuries, the **Chiesa di San Trovaso** (*Campo San Trovaso, €*) is noted for its double facades—one looming over the canal and the other above the square. Designed by one of Andrea Palladio's disciples, the design is distinctly Palladian, although the curved facades seem almost art deco. It's said the church was built this way in order to appease two wealthy, rival families that supported San Trovaso. The grotesque stone face at the bottom of the campanile is meant to scare away demons. Modestly adorned compared to many of the city's richly decorated churches, the interior of San Trovaso does offer paintings by Tintoretto and

The old wooden shipyard buildings at Squero di San Trovaso

other Renaissance artists. Directly in front of the church, the **Squero di San Trovaso** is a small but very active boatyard where many of the city's gondolas are repaired. For the best view of the boatyard, head to the Fondamenta Nani on the opposite side of the canal. A few steps north along the quay lies the new **Vitraria Glass +A Museum** (*Fondamenta Nani, 041 098 8122, €*). Housed in the 16th-century Palazzo Nani Mocenigo, the collection features anything made of glass—jewelry, carnival masks, and artistic bottles.

■ SAN SEBASTIANO

Another charming backwater of Dorsoduro is the area around **Chiesa di San Sebastiano** (*Campo San Sebastiano, 041 275 0462, €*). One of a number of Venetian churches constructed in gratitude to God for ending an epidemic of the bubonic plague, the 16th-century shrine is most renowned for its cycle of paintings by Paolo Veronese. The full scale of his work—ceilings, frescoes, and individual paintings—is on display in the church. Veronese is also buried there, beneath a striking bust of the artist. Works by Titian, Tintoretto, and other Renaissance masters complete San Sebastiano's creative ensemble. A bridge leaps across the Tolentini Canal and the entrance to a very narrow alley called the Calle Avogaria. The first turn on the left leads to the **Teatro a l'Avogaria** (*Corte Zappa, 041 099 1967, €–€€€*). Very popular with locals, this experimental theater was founded in 1969 by director Giovanni Poli and continues to present a wide array of obscure works both ancient and modern. Although most performances are in Italian, the theater does present English-language plays each year. In keeping with the avant-garde vibe, admission is by voluntary donation—whatever you feel inclined to pay.

■ GIUDECCA

Quiet and little explored, Giudecca comprises the sinuous archipelago on the other side of the water from San Marco and the Zattere promenade. The bell tower of the **Basilica di San Giorgio Maggiore** (*Isola di San Giorgio Maggiore, 041 522 78 27*) is well known, as is the posh **Cipriani Hotel** (*041 240 801*), but visitors rarely venture farther into the neighborhood. Tucked into the former convent school behind the church is **Le Stanze del Vetro** (*Isola di San Giorgio Maggiore, 041 522 9138, €€*), a slick indoor and outdoor exhibition space that showcases modern artists who have worked with glass. Vaporettos call on other stops along the Giudecca waterfront. The 16th-century **Chiesa del Santissimo Redentore** (*Campo del SS. Redentore, 041 275 0462, €*), which soars above the Giudecca Canal, is one of architect Andrea Palladio's most impressive works. Clearly inspired by ancient Rome, the classical facade gives way to a vast dome and twin campaniles—unusual for Venice. Every July, the church is the centerpiece of the **Festa del Redentore** (see p. 129), during which a temporary pontoon bridge connects the church and the Zattere. The former home and workshop of haute couture maestro **Mariano Fortuny** (*Fondamenta S. Biagio 805, 393 825 7651*) is now a showroom dispensing rich fabrics, furniture, and accessories. The factory is closed to the public, but the gardens can be visited via prior appointment. Those who have packed their board shorts or bikini can take a dip in the **Piscina Comunale di Sacca Fisola** (*Sacca Fisola, 041 528 5430, €€*), a public indoor pool reached by footbridge from the main part of Giudecca.

■ Isola di San Michele

Almost perfectly square, this island between Cannaregio and Murano provides a venue for Venice's largest cemetery and the city's first Renaissance church. Only the Gothic campanile remains from an early church that was reworked in the late 15th century into the **Chiesa di San Michele in Isola** *(Isola di San Michele, 041 522 4119, €),* a design by master architect Mauro Codussi that blends white Istrian stone and Venetian red brick into a harmonious whole that rises high above the shoreline. The church is dedicated to St. Michael the archangel, who stands at the gates of heaven, weighing souls on Judgment Day. However, it wasn't until much later (1807) that the island became a burial ground. The sprawling multidenominational cemetery is reached via the cloisters behind the church. Among its many occupants are composer Igor Stravinsky, poets Ezra Pound and Joseph Brodsky, mathematician Christian Doppler, and Don Salvador de Iturbide (a former prince of Mexico).

The cemetery on Isola di San Michele with the church of San Cristoforo in the background

Cannaregio

The northernmost *sestiere* in Venice, Cannaregio is also the second most extensive—a bustling district whose main artery is Strada Nova. This unusually broad street for Venice was in fact the work of French occupiers during the 18th and 19th centuries. The name "Cannaregio" derives from the *canne,* or reeds, that flourished in the marshes here before the reclamation work that saw the district expand. The area is residential for the most part—this district is historically home to the city's Jewish population— and is peppered with marvelous historic landmarks, among them, the church known locally as I Gesuiti and the Gothic canalside palace Ca' d'Oro, now operating as an art gallery. The vast lagoon opens out along the northeastern edge of the neighborhood, to the joy of the rowing clubs whose members can be seen day in, day out propelling their craft with long oars as per the local standing-up style. By night, the district comes alive with some of the best *bacari* (wine bars) that Venice has to offer.

○ **Many of the narrow canals in Cannaregio are flanked with houses painted in bright colors.**

CANNAREGIO

Cannaregio

A state-of-the-art bridge, medieval houses, and an exquisite marble church are among the highlights of this low-key neighborhood.

❶ Ponte della Costituzione (see p. 96) From Piazzale Roma, walk north across this dazzling contemporary steel-and-glass bridge spanning the Grand Canal.

❷ Ghetto
(see pp. 102–103) Head north to the two squares that form the heart of the medieval Ghetto. Admire the unusually tall houses. Cross the iron bridge north of the Campo del Ghetto Nuovo.

❸ Fondamenta della Misericordia (see pp. 96–97) Stroll east on this canalside walkway, lined with inviting local wine bars and eateries. Turn north onto Campo dei Mori.

CANNAREGIO   DISTANCE: APPROX. 2.75 MILES (4.5 KM)
TIME: APPROX. 8 HOURS   START: PIAZZALE ROMA

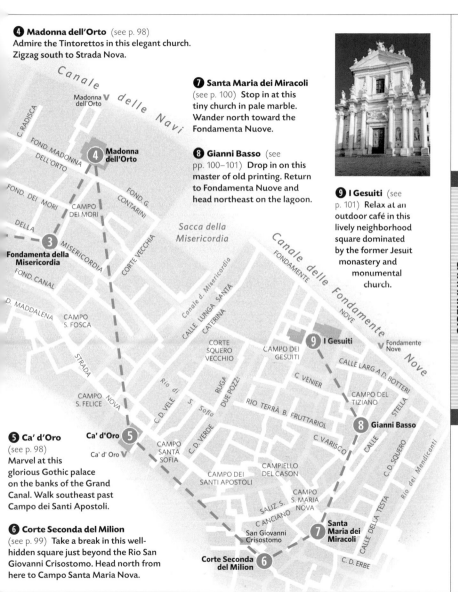

4 Madonna dell'Orto (see p. 98)
Admire the Tintorettos in this elegant church.
Zigzag south to Strada Nova.

7 Santa Maria dei Miracoli
(see p. 100) Stop in at this
tiny church in pale marble.
Wander north toward the
Fondamenta Nuove.

8 Gianni Basso (see
pp. 100–101) Drop in on this
master of old printing. Return
to Fondamenta Nuove and
head northeast on the lagoon.

9 I Gesuiti (see
p. 101) Relax at an
outdoor café in this
lively neighborhood
square dominated
by the former Jesuit
monastery and
monumental
church.

5 Ca' d'Oro
(see p. 98)
Marvel at this
glorious Gothic palace
on the banks of the Grand
Canal. Walk southeast past
Campo dei Santi Apostoli.

6 Corte Seconda del Milion
(see p. 99) Take a break in this well-
hidden square just beyond the Rio San
Giovanni Crisostomo. Head north from
here to Campo Santa Maria Nova.

CANNAREGIO

GOOD **EATS**

■ OSTERIA PARADISO PERDUTO
Affable chef Maurizio produces a delicious daily menu of seafood and vegetables, depending on availability from the city market. Live music. **Fondamenta della Misericordia 2540, 041 720 581, closed Tues., Wed., €€€**

■ OSTERIA ORTO DEI MORI
Book for memorable meals by creative Sicilian chef Lorenzo and a vast selection of wines from all over Italy. Enjoy your meal out in the square during summertime. **Campo dei Mori 3386, 041 524 3677, closed Tues., €€**

■ VINO VERO
If the stools at the window of this friendly wine bar are all occupied, sit yourself down at a canalside table with your glass of wine and *cicchetto* snack. **Fondamenta della Misericordia 2497, 041 275 0044, closed Mon., €**

Ponte della Costituzione

1 The white marble, steel, and glass Constitution Bridge soars over the northern end of the Grand Canal linking Piazzale Roma and the bus station with the city's train station and the Cannaregio district. Designed by Spanish architect Santiago Calatrava—the bridge is even known among locals as Ponte di Calatrava—this is the fourth bridge over the Grand Canal and the city's only new one since the years of fascism. Erected in 2008, the immense harp-like structure is 289 feet (88 m) long and affords wonderful views of the city. Assembled on the mainland, it was brought in at low tide so the barge transporting it could fit under the Accademia and Rialto bridges.

Piazzale Roma • Vaporetto: Piazzale Roma

Ghetto

2 (see pp. 102–103)
Campo del Ghetto Nuovo and Campo del Ghetto Vecchio • Vaporetto: Ponte delle Guglie

Fondamenta della Misericordia

3 True to its Venetian name, this *fondamenta* is a walkway running alongside the Misericordia Canal. Lined with houses, palaces, restaurants, and wine bars, this is the perfect place to stop for a light lunch. **Ostaria da Rioba** (*Fondamenta della Misericordia 2553, 041 524 4379, closed Mon., €€*), with its alfresco seating, is a good daytime option.

The Fondamenta della Misericordia took its name from the monumental **Scuola Nuova di Santa Maria della Misericordia** (*Campo della Misericordia*), a charitable confraternity, at the eastern end. Designed by Sansovino in 1534, it has since been used as barracks, a gym, and basketball arena, and is now an occasional exhibition venue. Past shows include a series of contemporary sculptures by Belgian artist Jan Fabre. Don't miss the curious shrine along the side of the building, which depicts the ferries that used to set sail from here bound for the northern islands. You'll also see a wooden bridge. This leads to an unusual, brick-paved courtyard and the arches of the elegant **Abbazia della Misericordia,** a former abbey now home to art restoration workshops. Movie fans should continue from the *scuola* and over the narrow bridge straight ahead: You'll recognize it from the 1973 film *Don't Look Now* starring Donald Sutherland. Close by is an especially old bridge—you will notice it lacks a parapet as all the city's bridges used to.

Rio della Misericordia • Vaporetto: Madonna dell'Orto

Locals stop for lunch on the Fondamenta della Misericordia.

Madonna dell'Orto

4 The tomb of the great Venetian Renaissance artist Jacopo Tintoretto can be seen inside this airy church. It also houses superb canvases by Tintoretto, including the "Presentation of the Virgin Mary in the Temple," and "The Last Judgment," reputedly his response to Michelangelo's work in the Sistine Chapel. The facade of the building features a statue of St. Christopher, patron saint of travelers, and was intended to protect the boatmen setting out across the lagoon to the outlying islands. Cross the bridge opposite into peaceful **Campo dei Mori** to see the curious statues of the *Mori* (Moors) embedded into corner columns. These so-called Moors, Rioba, Sandi, and Afani Mastelli, were in fact merchants from Morea in the Greek Peloponnese. Head around to the left corner of the square to view Tintoretto's house, marked with a plaque.

Campo Madonna dell'Orto • 041 719 933 • Entry by donation • Vaporetto: Campo della Madonna dell'Orto • madonnadellorto.org

Ca' d'Oro

5 Climb to the first-floor balcony for a close-up of the intricately decorated arched facade and slender marble columns of this splendid Gothic palace overlooking the Grand Canal. Amazingly, it was originally plastered in gold leaf—hence its name, House of Gold. Today, the building is home to the **Galleria Giorgio Franchetti,** named for the baron who devoted his resources to restoration before bequeathing it to the state in 1915. The collection features sculptures by Tullio Lombardo and "St. Sebastian" by Mantegna on the second floor—and Titian's "Venus" on the third floor. Don't miss the ground-floor paving—myriad geometrical designs using multicolored stone insets.

Calle Ca' d'Oro 3932 • 041 522 2349 • €€ • Vaporetto: Ca' d'Oro • cadoro.org

SAVVY **TRAVELER**

Keep an eye out for the free guided visits run by the **Ca' d'Oro** and included in the price of the entry ticket. One of the Italian state museums—along with the **Gallerie dell'Accademia** (see pp. 140–143) and **Palazzo Grimani** (see p. 37)—the Ca' d'Oro is free entry for the first Sunday of each month throughout the year to all visitors, Italians and foreigners alike.

Schoolchildren make sketches and paintings of the geometric paving at the Ca' d'Oro.

Corte Seconda del Milion

6 Covered passageways called *sotoportego* lead through to this hidden square with its own ancient wellhead and Gothic-style houses in the backstreets of Cannaregio. It is famous for its link with world-famous 13th-century Venetian explorer and navigator Marco Polo, and the name of the square is a reference to the million made-up stories he recounted in his memoirs. The adjoining **Teatro Malibran** (Malibran Theater; *Calle Maggioni, 041 786 603, €€€€€, teatrolafenice.it*) was reputedly constructed on the site of the family home. The theater was named for leading 19th-century Belgian-Spanish soprano Maria Malibran. The delightful premises are used by the famous Teatro La Fenice opera house and are the perfect setting for performances suited to a more intimate atmosphere.

Salizada San Giovanni Crisostomo • Vaporetto: Rialto, Ca' d'Oro

Santa Maria dei Miracoli

7 Seek out this tiny jewel box of a church dating back to the Renaissance period. Even if you don't enter the church, its facade offers plenty of pale-colored marble slabs and lunettes with insets to wonder at. It was constructed by 15th-century Tuscan architect Pietro Lombardo and his sons to house an icon said to have worked a miracle. One tradition claims that the facade is decorated with marble left over from the **Basilica di San Marco** (St. Mark's Basilica; see pp. 64–65). Inside, the coffered ceiling holds a series of portraits, while the steep altar steps bear intricate carvings. Santa Maria dei Miracoli belongs to the **Chorus Pass** scheme (see p. 176).

Campo dei Miracoli • Vaporetto stop: Fondamenta Nuove

Gianni Basso

8 In a narrow alley that leads through to the lagoon side and Fondamenta Nuove is this tiny *bottega,* an old-school printer's craft shop run by easygoing Gianni Basso. He learned his trade with the Armenian monks on the island of San Lazzaro, once a center par excellence for printing. Favored by celebrities, this talented artisan designs and hand-prints old-fashioned business cards, bookmarks, and writing paper, along with ex libris. He accepts bespoke orders and has a wide range of

The exquisite facade of Santa Maria dei Miracoli, also known as the Marble Church

beautifully crafted 19th-century
stamps from which to choose.

Calle del Fumo 5306 • 041 523 4681 • Closed
Sun. • Vaporetto: Fondamenta Nuove

I Gesuiti

9 Towering over the spacious
Campo dei Gesuiti that opens
onto the lagoon is the church of **Santa
Maria Assunta.** It is more commonly
known as I Gesuiti for the Jesuit
community who constructed it in the
early 18th century, after a 50-year ban
they earned for irritating the city.
Even before you step inside, you'll be
intimidated—by the giant statues
almost toppling off the front. In the
heavily baroque interior, spectacular
use is made of green and gray-white
inlaid stone decorating almost every
surface. Don't miss Titian's decidedly
gruesome "The Martyrdom of St.
Lawrence" near the entrance to the
church, the beautifully painted wooden
ceiling in the sacristy, or the forest of twisted
columns around the main altar.

**Part of the ceiling fresco in I Gesuiti,
depicting the assumption of Virgin Mary**

Next door, explore the peaceful cloisters of the sprawling
former monastery that now provides accommodation for university
students. Of an afternoon, the Campo dei Gesuiti is transformed
into a soccer field by the neighborhood children. There are also
benches, a drinking fountain, and several inviting cafés in which to
enjoy a gelato, drink, or a light meal at the end of your day.

Chiesa di Santa Maria Assunta, Campo dei Gesuiti • 041 528 6579 • Donations
welcome • Vaporetto stop: Fondamenta Nuove

Ghetto

The Ghetto in Venice occupies two Cannaregio squares. The term, now in common usage, derives from the iron foundry that once stood here.

Inside the 16th-century Levantine Synagogue in the Campo del Ghetto Vecchio

Although there are records of Jews living in the Veneto as of the fifth century, it was after 1492, in the wake of persecutions in Spain and Portugal, that groups found refuge in Venice. In March 1516, the Venetian Serenissima Republic declared that the city's Jews were to move to a limited area in the Cannaregio district—a good distance from the city's commercial and political center. That was 500 years ago. These days, the Jews of Venice live all over the city, although they return to the Ghetto for worship.

GHETTO LIFE

The Ghetto was enclosed by walls and gates that were locked at nighttime. If you enter the **Campo del Ghetto Nuovo** from Fondamenta di Cannaregio, you can see the holes in the stone doorposts that once held the wooden gates. You'll also see that the houses in this campo are unusually tall: Because of space limits, the buildings had to go upward so the apartment blocks have many stories with incredibly low ceilings. The Jews here were restricted to activities including medicine, dealing in secondhand clothes, and banking. Today, you can drop into an original Jewish pawnbrokers premises, **Banco Rosso.**

THE SYNAGOGUES

Each wave of refugees constructed their own *schola* (school) and synagogue—five survive and can be visited on the excellent guided tour (*in English, hourly from 10:30 a.m.*) organized through the **Museo Ebraico** (Jewish Museum; *041 715 359, closed Sat., Jan. 1, May 1, Dec. 25, and Jewish holidays, €€€, ticket price includes entry to the museum, museoebraico.it*). The oldest synagogues are the German structures dating back to 1528; the largest is the Spanish synagogue, constructed in 1575. However, the most atmospheric are the tiny rooftop temples with curious domes.

JEWISH CRAFTS

Today, the Ghetto is home to a number of shops selling Jewish crafts. **David's Shop** (*Campo del Ghetto Nuovo, 041 275 0418, closed Sat., davidshop.com*) sells handcrafted glass figurines of Jewish characters, glass candy, and even a glass chess set. **The Studio in Venice** (*Campo del Ghetto Vecchio, 041 520 8997*) offers delightfully illustrated portions of the Torah scrolls.

IN MEMORY

A landmark year was 1797, which saw the end of the Venetian Republic. French forces under Napoleon invaded the city and opened up the Ghetto. Peaceful times ensued, before the advent, centuries later, of Nazi-fascism. In 1943, a total of 200 Venetian Jews were deported to Auschwitz, and only eight returned. A poignant memorial on the northern wall of the Campo del Ghetto Nuovo lists all their names along with their ages.

Campo del Ghetto Nuovo and Campo del Ghetto Vecchio • Vaporetto: Ponte delle Guglie

The Palazzo

When Venice was at the height of its glory, each of the city's leading families had to own a palatial house, usually on the Grand Canal, to proclaim its wealth and status. Such a palazzo (palace) or *ca'* (short for *casa*—house) usually took the family name, as in Ca' Pesaro. Put to other uses today, these buildings provide intriguing glimpses of life during the Venetian golden age.

Palazzo Contarini Fasan, Cannaregio
Opposite: Canaletto's painting of the Grand Canal, looking southwest from the Rialto to Ca' Foscari (ca. 1725–1726)

The Merchant's Home

These Venetian families were merchants who owed their wealth to trade and were in no way ashamed of it. A palazzo therefore combined business with luxury living. Fronting the canal, the first floor was a warehouse alongside which boats docked to load and unload goods. The family lived directly above these storerooms on the *piano nobile* (noble floor). They had luxuriously furnished and decorated reception rooms and bedrooms, with tall windows and balconies overlooking the canal. Above this, the accommodation deteriorated with each move upward—at the top, the numerous servants were housed in the attics under the tiles.

From Riches to Rags

As wealth and pretension increased, the palaces built on the Grand Canal grew more extravagant. When Doge Francesco Foscari built his Ca' Foscari in the 15th century, he added a secondary piano nobile above the first, an innovation that soon became the norm. In the same period, the

Contarini family built the **Ca' d'Oro** (see p. 98), with an elaborate facade in the Gothic manner. In the 16th century, the Gothic gave way to a classical Renaissance style—the Palazzo Grimani is a fine example—and by the 17th century, when the **Ca' Pesaro** (see pp. 116–117) was built, palaces had grandiose baroque facades of Istrian stone.

The decline of the wealth and power of the great Venetian families brought an end to palace building. Through the 19th century, increasingly impoverished owners struggled to maintain their outsize mansions. Many were bought or rented by wealthy foreigners with artistic tastes. In the course of the 20th century, new uses were found for the palazzos, among them university buildings, apartments, hotels, and museums.

PALAZZO **FACADES**

Gothic (13th to 15th centuries) Look for facades with pointed arches and fine, lacelike tracery—see the **Doge's Palace** (pp. 66–67).

Renaissance (15th and 16th centuries) Palazzos have classical proportions and facades with rounded arches, and fluted columns, for example, **The Gritti Palace** hotel (see p. 32).

Baroque (17th century) Palazzos maintain classical proportions and have elaborate facades with all manner of stone carved swags, cherubs, and foliage. **Ca' Rezzonico** (see p. 138) is a good example of this.

CANNAREGIO

Bacari

A trip to Venice is not complete without a visit to one of the city's inviting *bacari* or *osterie*, typical wine bars dotted all over town. They do a brisk trade with the locals who drop in for a prelunch or predinner drink. These places tend to be small, and jostling for space is all part of the experience.

■ OSTERIA AL TIMON

The young clientele of this Cannaregio bar occupy the canal-front *fondamenta* (pavement) as well as two old traditional timber boats that are moored outside for extra seating. Immensely popular, the "rudder" bar serves rounds of crunchy toasted bread topped with marvelous combinations of cheese, tomato, salami, and grilled vegetables.

Fondamenta Ormesini 2754 • 041 524 6066 • € • Vaporetto: San Marcuola

■ UN MONDO DI VINO

Venture inside this former Cannaregio butcher's shop for a glass of Friuli wine to accompany a *polpetta di pesce* (fish rissole) or a Sicilian-style *sarda beccafico*—a fresh sardine that has been flattened, crumbed, and fried.

Salizada San Canciano 5984/A • 041 521 1093 • € • Closed Mon. • Vaporetto: Ca' d'Oro

■ OSTERIA CASA DEA CORTE

It's worth seeking out this Cannaregio establishment run by local greengrocer Oliver. Tables have been set up in the shady courtyard where you can relax with a drink and a plate of saltimbocca meatballs in a rich tomato sauce. Be courageous and go for *nervetti* (veal tendons) served with raw onion or a cocktail stick of *spienza* (sliced spleen).

Ramo del Magazen 1642 • 041 476 0612 • € • Vaporetto: San Marcuola

■ OSTERIA DAL RICCIO PEOCO

Cannaregio's "bald hedgehog" is a lively new bar run by a madcap crew. They specialize in live music and a delicious *panino* roll filled with soft salami. Balance your glass of wine and plate of food on the barrel outside and watch the world go by.

Campo dei Santi Apostoli 4462 • 041 241 0162 • € • Vaporetto: Ca' d'Oro

■ Ca' d'Oro alla Vedova

Renowned for its *polpette* (fried crumbed meatballs, sworn by all to be the best in town), Alla Vedova ("the widow's place") in Cannaregio has been serving wine for 130 years. Unless you book a table for a meal in the low-ceilinged premises hung with brass cooking pots, you'll be pressed around the glass-topped counter with the locals.

Calle del Pistor 3192 • 041 528 5324 • € • Vaporetto: Ca' d'Oro

■ Bacarando in Corte dell'Orso

The best way to find this place is to follow the public toilets signs from Campo San Bartolomeo in the San Marco *sestiere.* Around the corner and through a

WHAT **TO ORDER**

Ombra: a tumbler of house wine from a demijohn flask

Vino al calice: a glass selected from a blackboard list of bottled wines, mostly from the Veneto and neighboring Friuli regions

Spritz: a popular Venetian concoction of chilled white wine with fizzy water and a generous splash of aperitif (orange-red Campari Bitter, Select, or Aperol), adorned with a green olive and a slice of lemon or orange

Cicchetti: mouthwatering snacks on a counter display

CANNAREGIO

Customers enjoy wine and a light bite at Ca' d'Oro alla Vedova in Cannaregio.

Scallops served in their shells are among the dishes commonly served as *cicchetti*.

covered archway you'll find this friendly bar. The luscious display of *cicchetti* includes bite-size slices of French bread with creamy cheese and *sfilaceti*, which translates as dried horse meat, or *baccalà* (salted cod).

Sotoportego de l'Orso 5496 • 041 523 8280 • € • Vaporetto: Rialto

■ BACARO DA FIORE

This bustling family establishment just off Campo Santo Stefano in the San Marco neighborhood prides itself on its seafood dishes. Go to the counter to choose from the mesmerizing array of seasonal recipes. Depending on the time of year you will have the chance to taste *seppioline ai ferri* (grilled baby squid) or *moeche fritte* (tiny soft-shell crabs). Year-round staples here include *baccalà mantecato* (creamed salted cod) and *sarde in saor* (a Venetian standard that involves sardines marinated in vinegar and onion with the addition of currants and pine nuts). If these little dishes serve only to whet your appetite, why not request a table and stay on for dinner.

Calle de le Boteghe 3461 • 041 523 5310 • € • Vaporetto: San Samuele

■ Antica Osteria Ruga Rialto

Don't be put off by the rather dim atmosphere in this friendly place in the San Polo *sestiere*. Venetians flock here of an early evening, carefully timing their visit (6–7 p.m.) with the emergence of vast platters of *frittura mista di pesce* from the kitchen. Fragrant portions of battered fried squid, calamari, and fish are served on small plates to accompany a carafe of wine. It all happens under the watchful eye of the house cat reclining on a shelf in the middle of wine bottles.

Ruga Vecchia San Giovanni 692A • 041 521 1243
• € • Vaporetto: Rialto

■ Cantina Do Mori

Reputedly the oldest wine bar in Venice, dating back to 1462, these premises in San Polo are hung with old copper pans. House wine comes from the huge demijohns or selected bottles. The excellent *cicchetti* include cocktail sticks of baby octopus, artichoke chunks, tomatoes au gratin, grilled eggplant, and dried tomato.

Calle dei Do Mori 429 • 041 522 5401 • €
• Closed Sun. • Vaporetto: Rialto

■ Osteria alla Bifora

The beauty of this bar is its location in a lively square in the Dorsoduro *sestiere* that is popular with university students and Venetians alike. The name of the bar is a reference to its elegant arched window. Take a table and enjoy their trademark platter of flavorsome cold cuts of *prosciutto crudo* (Parma ham) and salami.

Campo Santa Margherita 2930 • 041 523 6119
• €€ • Vaporetto: Ca' Rezzonico

■ Cantina del Vino già Schiavi

Known locally as the Al Bottegon ("big shop"), this Dorsoduro bar sells quaffable wines and simple snacks such as mortadella sausage, pickles, and tiny soft bread rolls with sausage. The clientele usually spills out onto the canalside and adjoining bridge. Inside, a whole wall is given over to a wine display should you need a good bottle to take away with you.

Fondamenta Nani 992 • 041 523 0034 • €
• Vaporetto: Accademia

■ Osteria da Codroma

This laid-back establishment in Dorsoduro is frequented by students and staff from the nearby university. Once armed with a glass of wine and a plate of bar snacks, take a seat in the lovely timber-paneled premises and enjoy the attractive spread of photos of city life that covers the walls.

Fondamenta Briati 2540 • 041 524 6789
• € • Vaporetto: San Basilio

San Polo & Santa Croce

SAN POLO & SANTA CROCE

Nestled within the upper loop of the Grand Canal, the neighborhood of San Polo is the city's oldest. It was originally named Rivoaltus—literally meaning "high bank"—as this was the highest bank of land in the lagoon. The area was first settled in around A.D. 800, and by 1400, it was the commercial hub of the city. Among its major attractions are the Rialto Bridge and market to the east and, to the west, the magnificent Scuola Grande di San Rocco, home to the life's work of Tintoretto. Santa Croce boasts Ca' Pesaro, an exceptional modern art gallery, and Palazzo Mocenigo with its rich collection of Venetian costumes. These neighborhoods are also home to several fine churches, not least the Basilica di Santa Maria Gloriosa dei Frari, the Chiesa di San Giacomo dall'Orio, and the Chiesa di San Polo.

◀ **Locals relax at a café overlooking the Grand Canal in San Polo, just a stone's throw from the Rialto Market.**

San Polo & Santa Croce

*Enjoy the sights and sounds of market life and admire fine art
from Tintoretto and Titian to Klimt and Kandinsky.*

❸ Ca' Pesaro (see pp. 116–117) See the works of modern masters at this museum of modern art set in a 17th-century palazzo. Take a short walk northwest on Fondamenta de Ca' Pesaro then south on Fondamenta Mocenigo.

❹ Palazzo Mocenigo (see p. 117) Lust over the stunning costumes of the Venetian upper classes from times gone by. Continue west on Calle del Tintor then south on Calle Larga Rosa.

❺ Chiesa di San Giacomo dall'Orio (see p. 118) Enjoy the calm interior of this ancient church, thought to be named for a laurel tree (*alloro* in Italian) that once stood in the campo outside. Wend your way south to Campo San Rocco.

❻ Santa Maria Gloriosa dei Frari (see pp. 120–121) Marvel at this rich collection of art and sculpture that includes works by Bellini, Titian, Canova, and Donatello. The Scuola Grande di San Rocco is behind the church.

Canal

PONTE
D. SCALZI

CAMPIELLO
SAN SIMEON
PROFETA

RIVA DE

LISTA D. BARI

CAMPIELLO
DELLA
COMARE

CAMPO
NAZARIO
SAURO

S A N T A

C R O C E

FOND. RIO MARIN O. GARZOTTI

CORTE CANAL

FOND. RIO MARIN

CAMPO D. LANA

C. L.

CONTARINA RIO

C. D. LACA

C. CAMPAZZO

C. D. CHIOVERE

C. DIETRO
L'ARCHIVIO

C. FALIER

**Scuola Grande
di San Rocco** ❼

C. VINANTI

C. DEI PRETI CROSERA

CAMPIELLO
MOSCA

CAMPO SAN
PANTALON

C. LARGA FOSCARI

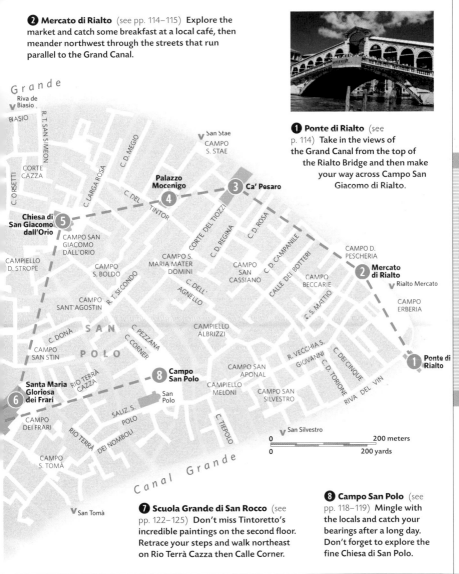

2 **Mercato di Rialto** (see pp. 114–115) Explore the market and catch some breakfast at a local café, then meander northwest through the streets that run parallel to the Grand Canal.

1 **Ponte di Rialto** (see p. 114) Take in the views of the Grand Canal from the top of the Rialto Bridge and then make your way across Campo San Giacomo di Rialto.

Grande

Riva de
v Biasio

BIASIO

R. T. SAN SIMEON

CORTE
CAZZA

C. ORSETTI

C. LARGA ROSA

C. D. MEGIO

v San Stae
CAMPO
S. STAE

**Palazzo
Mocenigo**

C. DEL TINTOR.

4

3 **Ca' Pesaro**

**Chiesa di
San Giacomo
dall'Orio** **5**

CAMPO SAN
GIACOMO
DALL'ORIO

CAMPIELLO
D. STROPE

CAMPO
S. BOLDO

CAMPO
SANT'AGOSTIN

R. T. SECONDO

CORTE DEL TIOZZI

C. D. REGINA

C. D. ROSA

CAMPO S.
MARIA MATER
DOMINI

C. DELL'
AGNELLO

CAMPO
SAN
CASSIANO

C. D. CAMPANILE

CALLE DEI BOTTERI

CAMPO
BECCARIE

R. S. MATTIO

CAMPO D.
PESCHERIA

2 **Mercato
di Rialto**

v Rialto Mercato

CAMPO
ERBERIA

S A N

P O L O

C. DONA

CAMPO
SAN STIN

C. PEZZANA

C. CORNER

CAMPIELLO
ALBRIZZI

**Santa Maria
Gloriosa
dei Frari** **6**

RIO TERRA
CAZZA

8 **Campo
San Polo**

San
Polo

CAMPO
SAN
APONAL

CAMPIELLO
MELONI

R. VECCHIA S.
GIOVANNI

C. DEL CINQUE

C. D. TORIONE

RIVA DEL VIN

CAMPO SAN
SILVESTRO

1 **Ponte di
Rialto**

CAMPO
DEI FRARI

SALIZ. S.
POLO

RIO TERRA DEI NOMBOLI

C. TIEPOLO

v San Silvestro

CAMPO
S. TOMÀ

Canal Grande

0			200 meters
0			200 yards

v San Tomà

7 **Scuola Grande di San Rocco** (see pp. 122–125) Don't miss Tintoretto's incredible paintings on the second floor. Retrace your steps and walk northeast on Rio Terrà Cazza then Calle Corner.

8 **Campo San Polo** (see pp. 118–119) Mingle with the locals and catch your bearings after a long day. Don't forget to explore the fine Chiesa di San Polo.

Ponte di Rialto

1 The Rialto Bridge is the oldest in Venice. A major symbol of the city, the bridge crosses the Grand Canal between the San Marco and San Polo *sestieri*. Originally constructed as a wooden drawbridge, the structure we see today—with a central stone archway supporting two rows of arch-fronted shops and three parallel, stepped walkways—was built in 1591. There are 24 shops in total, selling typical Venetian souvenirs, including glass, jewelry, leather, and silk goods. From the center point, you can catch beautiful views overlooking the Grand Canal in both directions. Just west of the bridge, along the banks of the canal, the **Riva del Vin** was named for the many wine cellars and merchants who used to ply their trade here, their boats laden with wine. Running parallel to this, **Calle dei Boteri** is where they made their barrels.

Riva del Vin • Vaporetto: Rialto Mercato

GOOD **EATS**

■ **ALL'ARCO**
A small *osteria* offering great *cicchetti* and wine at reasonable prices. Open until 2:30 p.m., it's the ideal place to stop after exploring the market. **Calle Arco 1451, 041 520 5666, €**

■ **AL PROSECCO**
Enjoy a light lunch in a lovely relaxed atmosphere. Salads and small dishes are on offer here, with alfresco seating in summer. **Campo San Giacomo dall'Orio 1503, 041 524 0222, €€**

■ **VINERIA ALL'AMARONE**
A personable family-run business with plenty of personality. Expect to find a great selection of cold cuts, cicchetti, pasta, and an excellent selection of wines. **Calle dei Sbianchesini 1131, 041 523 1184, closed Wed., €€**

Mercato di Rialto

2 The Rialto Market *(mornings only)* has been the epicenter of Venetian life since 1097. The market occupies a roughly rectangular area to the west of the **Ponte di Rialto** (Rialto Bridge). A riot of color, **Campo Cesare Battisti** is home to the fruit and vegetable market, bursting with seasonal produce. In springtime, you'll see asparagus, spring beans, and artichokes from San Erasmo; summer brings the intoxicating smell of fresh ripe strawberries and figs; and fall is rich with mushroom varieties, pumpkins, and fresh nuts. Proudly labeled, at least 80 percent of the stock is grown locally. Running parallel to the market stalls is a row of butcher's shops, including one (Macelleria Equina) that specializes in horse

A Rialto fishmonger proudly hoists his catch of the day.

meat. Beyond the fruit and veg, the fish market dominates **Campo della Pescheria** (*pescheria* means "where fish is sold" in Italian). Locals and restaurateurs come here for the freshest seafood in Venice—tiny anchovies, sweet-tasting mackerel, plump sea bass, and glistening squid, scallops, and baby octopus. The structure housing the fish market (*closed Mon., Sun.*) dates from 1905. Look to the tops of the columns to see carved fish heads and sea horses. You'll also see a marble tablet listing the legal sizes for selling fish. Although centuries old, these rules still apply today. Flanking the southern edge of the campo, the **Ruga dei Spezieri** was traditionally a street of spice merchants. Seek out the evocative **Drogheria Mascari** (see p. 40), with its beautiful window displays of dried herbs, spices, and specialty groceries.

Campo Cesare Battisti, Campo della Pescheria, and Campo Beccarie • Closed Sun. • Vaporetto: Rialto Mercato

A monumental plaster mask at Ca' Pesaro, the creation of Italian sculptor Adolfo Wildt (1903)

Ca' Pesaro

3 This magnificent palazzo was built by the Pesaro family during the 17th century; it is now the home of the **Galleria Internazionale d'Arte Moderna** (Museum of Modern Art). A haven for art lovers, this extensive collection of modern art ranges from the beginning of the 20th century to the end of the 1960s and includes works by artists such as Wassily Kandinsky, Paul Klee, Henry Moore, Henri Matisse, and Gustav Klimt. Exhibited within 15 rooms on the first floor of the building, the art is arranged thematically as well as chronologically. For example, Room 4 discusses expressions of symbolism and secession that dominated the early 20th century and features Klimt's striking portrait, "Giuditta II." Emil Nolde's "Piante Fiorite" is one of several works that considers the exploration of color during the 1930s and 1940s in Room 9. Room 11 looks at the surrealism and abstraction of the

1950s and features the work of Kandinsky, Klee, and Max Ernst. The collection also features works by Venetian painters from the 19th and 20th centuries, significant works from the Biennale (see p. 82) in its very early years, and a large sculpture collection. The second floor of the palazzo is used to house temporary exhibitions; on the third floor, you will find the **Museo d'Arte Orientale** (Oriental Art Museum; *41 524 1173, arteorientale.org*) with an important collection of Japanese art from the Edo period alongside Indonesian and Chinese Art.

Fondamenta de Ca' Pesaro 2076 • 041 721 127 • €€€ • Closed Mon., Jan. 1, Dec. 25 • Vaporetto: San Stae • capesaro.visitmuve.it

Palazzo Mocenigo

4 The Mocenigo Palace is the former home of one of the most important Venetian families. This particular family provided the city with 10 doges over a 400-year period, its importance further reflected in the fact that no fewer than 12 palaces in the city bear the family name. This particular palace in San Stae, an expanded and renovated Gothic building, houses the **Centro Studi di Storia del Tessuto e del Costume** (Study Center for the History of Textiles and Costumes), which occupies some 15 rooms on the first floor. Among the many textiles on display here, you'll see a collection of exquisite 18th-century dresses (Room 6), rare and valuable 13th- and 14th-century fabrics, woven with gold and silver thread (Room 7), and period menswear (Room 11). Each of the rooms is decorated in 17th- and 18th-century style— including portraits of the Mocenigo family—and it is impossible to visit without getting a taste for the luxurious lifestyle of the Venetian nobility.

Fondamenta Mocenigo 1992 • 041 721 798 • €€ • Closed Mon., Jan. 1, Dec. 25 • Vaporetto: San Stae • mocenigo .visitmuve.it

IN **THE KNOW**

Rooms 13–19 at Palazzo Mocenigo are dedicated to the history of perfume. Room 14 houses the laboratory of a 16th-century perfumer, with displays of raw materials and perfume-making processes. Room 16 holds a display of rare perfume vials and containers spanning several millennia. Best of all, in Room 17 is a collection of 24 essences with which visitors can experiment to make scents of their own.

During the 15th century, the front entrance to the **Chiesa di San Polo** was blocked off and filled in with the buildings you see here today. The main entrance is now located along one side of the church. As you approach **Campo San Polo** from San Tomà, look for a narrow alleyway to the left, just before reaching the church. Follow this alleyway to a little courtyard and head up the stairs there to catch a glimpse of the church's original facade and center rose dating from A.D. 837.

Chiesa di San Giacomo dall'Orio

5 San Giacomo dall'Orio is one of the oldest churches in Venice, its original building having been founded during the 10th century. It was later rebuilt in 1225 and further modified during the 15th and 16th centuries, so the present-day church is an eclectic mix of styles. On entering the building you will notice the Gothic "ship's-keel" wooden ceiling. There are also a few other interesting treasures to be found inside, notably Lorenzo Lotto's main altarpiece, "Virgin Mary and Child with Apostles and Saints" (1546). The old sacristy features two paintings by Palma il Giovane—both created ca. 1581—which depict scenes from the Old Testament. To the right of the altar, you'll see a sixth-century green granite column that came from Byzantium.

Campo San Giacomo dall'Orio • 041 275 0462 • Closed Sun. • Vaporetto: Riva de Biasio • chorusvenezia.org

Santa Maria Gloriosa dei Frari

6 (see pp. 120–121)

Campo San Rocco 3072 • 041 272 8611 • € • Vaporetto: San Tomà • chorusvenezia.org

Scuola Grande di San Rocco

7 (see pp. 122–125)

Campo San Rocco 3052 • 041 523 4864 • €€€ (includes free audio guide) • Closed Jan. 1, Dec. 25 • Vaporetto: San Tomà

Campo San Polo

8 Campo San Polo is the second largest square in Venice. The entire square was originally covered with grass—cattle used to graze here and vibrant markets were held once a week. It was paved in 1493 and, in the years following, it has hosted many festivals and events, including bull fights, masked balls, celebrations, dances, fairs, and markets. More recently, the campo hosts an annual winter ice rink. Originally, a canal ran straight through the campo just beside Palazzo Soranzo. Take a look, and you can see where the canal ended abruptly at one end of the square and took up again at the other. The church in the southwest corner of the campo, with its back facing into the square, is the **Chiesa di San Polo** (Church of San Polo; €, *closed Sun.*). Opposite the entrance to the church is the bell tower, at the base of which are two interesting carved lions—one grasping a human head and the other fighting a serpent-like creature. If you have time, step inside the church, to see "The Stations of the Cross" by Tiepolo and "The Last Supper" by Tintoretto.

Salita San Polo • Vaporetto: San Tomà

Head to the southeast corner of Campo San Polo for shady cafés and bars.

Santa Maria Gloriosa dei Frari

The final resting place of the great artist of the Venetian school, Titian, this church is also home to one of his most famous works.

The tomb of Antonio Canova, Venice's renowned neoclassical sculptor

The Basilica of Santa Maria Gloriosa dei Frari has had many expansions since it was first built in 1222. What you see today is a very large Gothic structure with the second highest campanile (bell tower) in the city and a large cloister. Enter the church via the main entrance, and the first thing that will strike you is the sheer size and height of its 335-foot (102 m) nave. The vast interior provides the perfect backdrop against which to exhibit the immense and important works that attract so many visitors.

SAN POLO & SANTA CROCE

■ TOMBS AND MONUMENTS

Canova's tomb will capture your attention first with its unique pyramid-like structure. Its pinnacle meets a small window, which appears brightly illuminated and gives you the impression that the tomb itself is connecting with the light of the universe. The statues on either side are those of an angel, representing safe passage of Canova's soul, and a winged lion with a book, representing the wisdom the artist takes with him. Directly opposite Canova's tomb is a monument to Titian, created by one of Canova's pupils, Luigi Zandomeneghi, in 1852. Titian is centered in the piece, surrounded by bas-reliefs of some of his greatest works. Hopping back to the other side, there is a monument to Doge Giovanni Pesaro by Baldassare Longhena. Four slaves support the upper part of the monument that carries the doge, which is adorned with symbols of religion, virtue, justice, and understanding.

■ THE APSE

Continue through to the apse, passing Titian's **"Madonna of Ca' Pesaro"** and the **Monks Choir**. The latter is the

only one in Venice to remain intact. The work of Marco Cozzi, a master wood carver, each of the structure's 124 seats features intricate carving and inlaid decoration. Within the apse, dominating the high altar, is Titian's masterpiece, "The Assumption of the Virgin" (1518), monumental in scale and with a rich, gold background, before which Mary, robed in red, is raised up to God by cherubs.

■ SACRISTY AND CHAPTER ROOM

More great works can be seen in the eastern wing of the church. In the sacristy you'll see the "Madonna and Saints," by Giovanni Bellini (1488). Beyond, in the chapter room, is Paolo Veneziano's "Madonna With Child, St. Francis, and St. Elizabeth" (1339).

SAN POLO & SANTA CROCE

Campo San Rocco 3072 • 041 272 8611 • € • Vaporetto: San Tomà • chorusvenezia.org

Scuola Grande di San Rocco

This institution dedicated to helping the poor is literally covered in great works by the Venetian artist Tintoretto.

The handsome facades of the Scuola Grande di San Rocco (left) and Chiesa di San Rocco (right)

You don't have to be an art lover to appreciate the sheer splendor of the Scuola Grande di San Rocco—it is impossible not to marvel at its magnificence. In Venice there were six main *scuole,* each dedicated to a different patron saint and run by a civil organization with around 500 members. The Scuola Grande di San Rocco is dedicated to St. Roch, who very aptly was a protector against the plague, of which Venice, being a very busy port, had its fair share. Tintoretto and Titian are both said to have succumbed to a death by plague.

THE BUILDING

Under the guidance of three different architects, this stunning white marble and Istrian stone Renaissance building was completed ca. 1560, after 50 years in the making. A glance at the facade before entering reveals the work of each architect. Pietro Bon created the lower portion of the main facade, while the upper level was designed by Scarpagnino. Look closely at the shapes and styles of the windows and their different styles become evident. On the ground floor, the windows are Romanesque in design, typical of the early Renaissance, while above, the windows are more neoclassical. The south facade is later and was created by Sante Lombardo and his father, Tullio.

ASSEMBLY HALL

A large, open, rectangular room with a wooden beamed ceiling dominates the ground floor. The hall itself contains two sets of octagonal white marble columns that lead to an altar dedicated to San Rocco, patron saint of the institution. There are eight large works by Tintoretto on this floor, depicting the early life of Christ and the life of the Virgin Mary. To the right, two staircases converge at the **Scarpagnino Staircase,** with its vaulted ceiling and painted walls.

SCARPAGNINO STAIRCASE

Along the left wall of the staircase you will find "**The Madonna Saves Venice From the Plague of 1630**" by Pietro Negri. It illustrates the deadly plague that wiped out one-third of Venetians and resulted in the building of **Santa Maria della Salute** (see pp. 134–135). Opposite is another painting with a plague theme, Antonio Zanchi's "**The Virgin Appears to the Plague Victims.**" The paintings lead up to the **Sala Grande** and **Tesoro.**

SALA GRANDE

The Great Hall will take your breath away, for every surface is richly decorated. As you enter the room to your right, you have an altar with two paintings on easels. They are Titian's "**The Annunciation**" (1559–1564) and "**The Visitation,**" painted by Tintoretto in 1588. The room is lined with striking wooden carved figures

The Scarpagnino Staircase with Zanchi's painting depicting Venetian plague scenes

created by Francesco Pianta il Giovane that represent themes such as Hope, Fury, Faith, Honor, and Ignorance. The order starts on the east wall and runs around to the right. Above these allegorical figures, and arranged in 11 panels, are a series of paintings by Tintoretto. Viewed chronologically, they tell the story of the New Testament from **"The Adoration of the Shepherds"** to **"The Temptation of Christ."** The ceiling also contains Tintoretto paintings, this time depicting scenes from the Old Testament, starting with **"Original Sin"** and ending with **"Passover, Daniel Is Saved by the Angel."** Pick up a large mirror in the center of the room, which will allow you to view the ceiling without stretching your neck. Two other notable works in this grand salon are **"Agar and Ishmael Succoured by the Angel"** and **"Abraham Visited by the Angels,"** both painted by Tiepolo in 1782.

■ SALA DELL'ALBERGO

The Sala dell'Albergo is to the left off the Great Hall. This is the room that contains Tintoretto's winning entry, the central painting **"San Roch in Glory."** The paintings surrounding the work represent the other main scuole of Venice, while the corners represent

A total of 21 works by Tintoretto cover the ceiling of the Great Hall alone.

the four seasons. Wrapping around the walls are large canvases depicting the Passion and the death of Christ.

■ TESORO

The Treasury on the top floor of the scuola is a small room containing an impressive collection of chalices, crucifixes, and reliquaries. These masterpieces of the goldsmith's craft are richly decorated with ornaments and jewels.

■ QUADRERIA

The Quadreria contains a fine collection of paintings, furniture, and ceramics—donations, primarily from former members of the scuola. The works are very diverse and originate from all over the world. Giacomo Bisacco Palazzi, one of the most significant donors, was an avid collector and part of his ceramics collection is on display here, including pieces of 18th-century Italian majolica.

Campo San Rocco 3052 • 041 523 4864 • €€€ (includes free audio guide) • Closed Jan. 1, Dec. 25 • Vaporetto: San Tomà

Carnevale

From modest beginnings, Carnevale (Carnival) developed into the biggest and longest annual party in Europe. By the 18th century, as many as 30,000 visitors thronged the city's narrow streets in the weeks before Lent, attending masquerades and balls, showing off extravagant costumes, gambling, and conducting illicit affairs, all from behind the anonymity of the mask.

A joker poses at the Venice Carnevale.
Opposite: An artist adds the finishing touches to a mask at the Ca' Macana workshop.

Carnevale celebrations began as a pre-Lent feast and developed into a series of hedonistic events in the weeks leading up to Ash Wednesday. During the 15th century, groups of young noblemen, known as *compagnie di calze* (stocking groups, because of their brightly colored stockings), took over organizing the main events. Carnival-goers enjoyed processions, opera and theater, and masked balls. Finally, on Shrove Tuesday, **Piazza San Marco** (St. Mark's Square; see pp. 58–59) was filled with crowds singing and dancing all day.

"Good Day, Madam Mask"

Masks and costumes have always been a central feature of Carnevale, acting as social levelers and allowing people to enjoy themselves in complete anonymity, the cardinal rule being that you never investigate a person's identity. The familiar *bauta* outfit, worn by men, consisted of a white mask worn with a three-cornered hat and black cloak. Women wore the *moretta*, a black velvet mask that covered most of the face, with a veil and small hat.

SAN POLO & SANTA CROCE

Theatrical commedia dell'arte characters were also popular, including the half-mask Columbine, the maidservant, and the multicolored, diamond-patterned *arlecchino* (harlequin).

Decline and Reinvention

During the 18th century, as the republic went into decline, Carnival celebrations became more hectic and extravagant. Visitors from all over Europe joined the locals to party all night. When the republic ended in 1797, the new Austrian government banned the event. There were a few short-lived revivals, but it was not until 1978 that the event was firmly reestablished. It now lasts for 10 days, beginning with the Flight of the Angel, performed by an acrobat who descends upside down along a rope from the belfry in San Marco to the loggia of the Palazzo Ducale. This is followed by processions on the canals, costume parades, masked balls, and a party in Piazza San Marco on Shrove Tuesday.

Venetian Festivals

A number of magnificent festivals take place throughout the year, and if you would like to be part of something very typically Venetian, it is worth planning your trip to coincide with one of these events. Since Venice is a city of water, some of the best celebrations take place on the canals.

■ FESTA DI SAN GIACOMO DALL'ORIO
For 10 days each July, the Campo San Giacomo Dall'Orio is completely transformed with lights, banners, and row upon row of long tables and benches. A large food stall offers ribs, chicken, sausages, meatballs, pasta dishes, and polenta. Held in aid of the homeless and needy, this charitable festival has been running since 1966.

San Polo • Mid-July • Vaporetto: Riva de Biasio

■ HISTORICAL REGATTA
The historical regatta is believed to have its origins in the mid-13th century. The event usually begins at 4 p.m. with a procession of historical boats with costumed rowers. Four races follow, each with a different category, depending on the type and age of the vessels. The race starts in Castello, crosses the Bacino San Marco, and sweeps down the Grand

Canal until reaching the area that once contained the Santa Chiara Convent. Vessels then return to the finishing line at Ca' Foscari in Dorsoduro. Expect to see hundreds of people cheering the competitors on and a parade of spectacular traditional boats and costumes. For the best views, station yourself anywhere between the Rialto and San Tomà vaporetto stops.

Grand Canal • 1st Sun. in Sept. • Vaporetto: Rialto, San Tomà • regatastoricavenezia.it

■ FESTA DELLA MADONNA DELLA SALUTE
Every year, Venetians gather to light a candle at this festival in honor of Our Lady of Health. The event originated in 1630 as a prayer procession to Mary, asking for relief from the great plague that was ravaging the city at the time. In return for deliverance, the doge vowed to build a church— **Santa Maria della Salute** (see

Fireworks blaze over the Rialto Bridge at Christmas.

pp. 134–135). Today, a temporary wooden bridge crosses over the Grand Canal from **Santa Maria del Giglio** (*Campo Santa Maria del Giglio, 041 275 0462, chorusvenezia.org*) in San Marco. Families gather to eat *castradina*, a dish of mutton with cabbage, onion, and wine.

Santa Maria della Salute • Nov. 21
• Vaporetto: Salute

■ FESTA DEL REDENTORE
This weekend celebration gives thanks for the deliverance from another plague that broke out, this time in the mid-16th century. Originally, a bridge of barges would link the Zattere in Dorsoduro with the island of Giudecca and the doge would lead a procession across to the church. Nowadays, a temporary wooden bridge links the two islands and people gather in the Bacino San Marco in their decorated boats with wine and picnics. Celebrations include a stunning firework display on the Saturday evening and traditional religious ceremonies on the Sunday.

San Marco Basin • 3rd Sun. in July
• Vaporetto: Salute

Dorsoduro

Wedged between the Grand Canal and the Canale della Giudecca to the south of Venice, Dorsoduro derives its rather odd name ("hard backbone") from the fact that it was one of the few solid landmasses emerging from the Venice lagoon. After more than a thousand years of urbanization, the *sestiere* is renowned for its split personality—laid-back residential area by day, boisterous nightlife enclave after dark. But more than anything else, Dorsoduro is known for art. The founding of the Accademia di Belle Arti di Venezia (Academy of Fine Art) in the mid-18th century paved the way for a creative legacy that also includes the Peggy Guggenheim Collection of contemporary art, the sumptuous Ca' Rezzonico palace with its 18th-century treasures, and the Punta della Dogana museum with its edgy, ultramodern exhibitions. When all of that art starts to overwhelm, this neighborhood offers plenty of spots for quiet reflection among its many *campi* (squares) and canalside walks.

◐ **Tables spill out into the Campo Santa Margherita at the Albergo Antico Capon restaurant.**

Dorsoduro

See art from the Middle Ages through modern times on an amble through this slender sestiere tucked between the Grand and Giudecca Canals.

❻ Gallerie dell'Accademia (see pp. 140–143)
Five hundred years of Venetian creative genius fill the galleries of the city's paramount art museum. Take a vaporetto from outside the museum one stop to Ca' Rezzonico.

❼ Ca' Rezzonico (see p. 138) **See** 18th-century Venice via artworks and furnishings arranged as if a wealthy merchant family still lived here. Follow Calle del Traghetto to Campo San Barnaba, cross over the canal and continue on Rio Terà Canal.

❽ Campo Santa Margherita (see p. 139) Browse the market stalls or relax in one of the many bars or outdoor cafés, often crowded with students from the nearby universities.

0 —————————— 200 meters
0 —————————— 200 yards

DORSODURO DISTANCE: APPROX. 1.25 MILES (2 KM)
TIME: APPROX. 7–8 HOURS START: SALUTE VAPORETTO PIER

DORSODURO

⑤ Ponte dell'Accademia (see pp. 137–138) This beloved wooden span provides a great perch to take a selfie or simply gaze at the Grand Canal. Cross the Campo della Carità.

④ Chiesa dei Gesuati (see p. 137) Rococo runs amok inside this flamboyant baroque church with its masterpieces by Tiepolo, Tintoretto, and Morlaiter. From beside the church, follow Rio Terrà Foscarini back across the island.

③ The Zattere (see p. 136) Linger as long as you like on the stunning waterfront promenade that runs nearly a mile along the north shore of the Giudecca Canal. The Gesuati church is located about halfway along.

② Collezione Peggy Guggenheim (see p. 135) Revel in Peggy Guggenheim's jaw-dropping compendium of 20th-century masters as well as the view of the Grand Canal from the back terrace. Trek Calles Molin and Monastero south, crossing the island to reach the Giudecca Canal.

① Santa Maria della Salute (see pp. 134–135) Start the day at Salute's landmark baroque church, filled with masterpieces by Titian and Tintoretto. Cross the bridge over the Salute Canal and head west on Calles Bastion and Barbaro.

DORSODURO

Map labels:
Canal Grande
Accademia
⑤ Ponte dell'Accademia
⑥ Gallerie dell'Accademia
Collezione Peggy Guggenheim
② CPO. SAN VIO
RIO TERRÀ A. FOSCARINI
FOND. VENIER
FONDAMENTA BRAGADIN
CAMPO SANT' AGNESE
RIO TERRÀ SAN VIO
FOND. SORANZO D. FORNACE
FOND. DI CA' BALÀ
Salute
CAMPO D. SALUTE
① Santa Maria della Salute
C. D. SQUERO
FONDAMENTA ZATTERE AI SALONI
Zattere ③
F. ZATTERE ALLO SPIRITO SANTO
Spirito Santo

Santa Maria della Salute

1 Rising high above the eastern tip of Dorsoduro at the confluence of the Giudecca and Grand Canals, the Salute church is a tribute to both the indelible faith and artistic brilliance of Venice. Like the city's other "plague churches," this baroque basilica was erected in thanks to the Virgin Mary for deliverance from an outbreak of the bubonic plague that started in 1630 and went on to claim one-third of the city's population. Baldassare Longhena's offbeat octagonal design was suffused with symbolism. Before entering, stop to admire the impressive facade. Finished with white Istrian stone, the structure is based on a Roman triumphal arch and soars to a massive cupola that represents the crown of Mary. Pass through the gigantic bronze doors and into the vast interior. Eight chapels surround a luminous nave with an Escher-like geometric floor that converges on a vortex thought to have

The dome of Santa Maria della Salute is encircled by statues of saints and angels.

mystical curative properties. One of Venice's most lavishly decorated churches, the basilica is blessed with numerous Titian masterpieces—look up to see his dramatic Old Testament ceiling murals. You'll also see Tintoretto's "Marriage at Cana," Palma the Younger's marvelous take on Jonah emerging from the mouth of the whale, and "The Queen of Heaven Expelling the Plague" by Flemish sculptor Josse de Corte.

Fondamenta Salute • 041 241 1018 • € • Vaporetto: Salute • basilicasalutevenezia.it

Collezione Peggy Guggenheim

2 American heiress and art patron Peggy Guggenheim purchased a run-down waterfront palace—the Palazzo Venier dei Leoni—on the Grand Canal in 1948 and magically transformed it over the next 30 years into a showcase for modern art. From Duchamp and Dalì to Picasso, Chagall, Miró, and Kandinsky, the interior and alfresco areas of Peggy's former home are filled with paintings and sculptures by many of the masters of the 20th century. Among the many treasures you'll see here are the "Voice of Space" by René Magritte, "The Clarinet" by Georges Braque, "The Moon Woman" by Jackson Pollock, and "Magic Garden" by Paul Klee, as well as several works by Max Ernst (Peggy's second husband). Take a break in the museum café before admiring the works of Henry Moore, Barbara Hepworth, and Yoko Ono, among others, that are on display in the surrealist **Nasher Sculpture Garden.** The Peggy Guggenheim Collection also contains photography, cartoons, etchings, and jewelry, as well as pieces from Africa, Asia, the Pacific, and the Americas that aptly demonstrate how primitive art influenced the modern masters.

Calle Chiesa 701–704 • 041 240 5411 • Closed Tues. • €€€€ • Vaporetto: Salute • guggenheim-venice.it

IN **THE KNOW**

Twice a year, Dorsoduro is a venue for religious festivals during which temporary wooden votive bridges are built across the canals on either side of the *sestiere* (see pp. 128–129). The practice dates back to the Middle Ages when devotees flocked to **Santa Maria della Salute** and **Chiesa del Santissimo Redentore** (Church of the Most Holy Redeemer; *Campo del Santissimo Redentore, closed Sun., €*) to give thanks for ending outbreaks of the plague in Venice.

DORSODURO

The Zattere

3 This popular waterfront walk runs almost a mile (1.6 km) along the southern shore of Dorsoduro. Renowned for its incredible views across the water to Giudecca, the promenade is also spangled with bars, cafés, and restaurants, many with alfresco seating. Among the many historic buildings on the Zattere are the 17th-century Palazzo Ficquelmont-Clary (a longtime bastion of Austro-Hungarian nobles) and the Accademia di Belle Arti di Venezia school of the arts (housed in a 16th-century complex that once served as a hospital for patients deemed incurable). The latter hosts many events throughout the year, including art exhibitions and fashion shows. Grandest of the churches found along the Zattere is the **Chiesa dei Gesuati.**

Dorsoduro shoreline between Punta della Dogana and the Tolentini Canal
• Vaporetto: Zattere, San Basilio, Spirito Santo

Locals are drawn to the Zattere for their *passeggiata*—an evening or Sunday stroll.

Chiesa dei Gesuati

4 Officially this waterfront church is called **Santa Maria del Rosario** (St. Mary of the Rosary). But locals are more apt to call it I Gesuati ("The Jesuates"), a moniker first used in the 17th century when the property was transferred from the defunct Jesuate order (no relation to the Jesuits) to the Dominican brothers. Architect Giorgio Massari was commissioned to build a new church on the site, a project that stretched over two decades starting in 1724. See how the neoclassical facade mimics Andrea Palladio's somber **Chiesa del Santissimo Redentore** (Church of the Most Holy Redeemer; see p. 135) on the opposite shore of the Giudecca Canal. Step inside the building to find an interior that is pure rococo, a flamboyance that reaches a peak in the ceiling frescoes by Giambattista Tiepolo, which depict scenes from the life of St. Dominic. Another masterpiece is Tintoretto's poignant "Crucifixion." Nearly all of the monumental marble sculptures are by Giovanni Maria Morlaiter—figures that include Moses, Abraham, and the Baptism of Christ lend the church even more gravitas.

Fondamenta delle Zattere 918 • 041 275 0462 • Closed Sun. • € • Vaporetto: Zattere • chorusvenezia.org

IN **THE KNOW**

Perched at the eastern end of the Zattere promenade, the Punta della Dogana offers one of the best spots in Venice to ogle St. Mark's waterfront. It's also one of the city's art hubs. The triangular 17th-century Dogana di Mare (Customs House) that once monitored Venice's maritime trade is now home to the **Punta della Dogana Museum of Contemporary Art** (*Campo San Samuele 3231, 041 271 9031, €€€€*), which stages cutting-edge exhibits from the expansive postmodern collection of French tycoon François-Henri Pinault.

Ponte dell'Accademia

5 Named for the adjacent **Gallerie dell'Accademia** (Academy Galleries; see pp. 140–143), this beloved bridge is one of only four that span the Grand Canal. Take in the view looking eastward down the Grand Canal to **Santa Maria della Salute** church—it is one of the most photographed and painted scenes in the city. The current bridge is a replica of a former wooden version that once leaped the waterway at this spot. Designed in the 1930s by

DORSODURO

Eugenio Miozzi, the Brescia-born engineer who also restored the **Teatro La Fenice** (Venice Opera House; see pp. 61–62), the bridge was in a state of dilapidation until reconstruction was undertaken in the mid-1980s.

Campo della Carità • Vaporetto: Accademia

Gallerie dell'Accademia

6 (see pp. 140–143)

Campo della Carità 1050 • 041 520 0345 • €€€€ • Vaporetto: Accademia • gallerieaccademia.org

GOOD **EATS**

■ **AI ARTISTI**
An ideal *osteria* for a light lunch, *cicchetti* include grilled vegetables, marinated fish, and local cheeses. Alfresco seating. **Fondamenta della Toletta 1169/A, 041 523 8944, closed Sun., €€**

■ **BAR ALLA TOLETTA**
Midway between Gallerie dell'Accademia and Ca' Rezzonico, this bar has a range of grilled panini and freshly made sandwiches. **Calle della Toletta 1192, 41 520 01 96, €**

■ **LA PISCINA**
Tempura scallops with truffles, Sicilian shrimp with asparagus, and champagne black risotto with scampi are on the menu at this upscale seafood eatery. **Fondamenta delle Zattere 780, 041 241 3889, €€€€**

Ca' Rezzonico

7 Behind its baroque facade, the sublime Rezzonico Palace houses a museum dedicated to the splendor and decadence of 18th-century Venice. Once home to the Rezzonico family, subsequent residents include American artist John Singer Sargent and composer Cole Porter. The museum centers on a "lived-in" concept with furnishings arranged as if the palace were still occupied. Among the many highlights are the incredible ceiling frescoes of the **Nuptial Allegory Room** and **Throne Room,** the 17th-century Flemish weavings that decorate the **Tapestry Room,** Pietro Longhi's humorous and satirical portraits of ordinary Venetians, the majolica vases of the **Ai do San Marchi Pharmacy,** and the Venetian masters of the **Egidio Martini Picture Gallery.** Also worth noting are views of the Grand Canal from the palace's upper-story windows.

Fondamenta Rezzonico • 041 241 0100 • Closed Tues. • €€€ • Vaporetto: Ca' Rezzonico • carezzonico.visitmuve.it

DORSODURO

Visitors to Ca' Rezzonico attend a concert during Carnevale.

Campo Santa Margherita

8 Dorsoduro's liveliest square, this spacious campo attracts locals to its daily fruit, fish, and clothing stalls, and students from the nearby universities to its bars and outdoor cafés. It's one of the best places in the city to watch Venetians going about their everyday lives. Buskers and street musicians frequent the square, which also hosts the occasional concert or Carnevale (see pp. 126–127) event. The campo's primary raison d'être is to provide a space for chilling out. Relish a cappuccino at the **Caffè Rosso** *(041 528 7998, €)*, a spritz at the **Margaret Duchamp** bar *(041 528 6255, €)*, or an ice cream from the **Gelateria il Doge** *(Rio Terrà Canal, 041 523 460)*. Stay long enough and the mood changes from the mellow day crowd to the after-dark denizens who party long after midnight.

Calle della Chiesa • Vaporetto: Ca' Rezzonico, San Tomà

Gallerie dell'Accademia

*The iconic Academy Gallery offers a visual encyclopedia
of Venetian art from the 14th through 18th centuries.*

Two of the eight large canvases that make up the "Miracles of the Relic of the True Cross"

Anchored to the south bank of the Grand Canal, the Academy collection
covers everything from the late-Byzantine and Gothic periods through the
Renaissance and baroque. All of the great masters are here—Bellini, Veronese,
Tintoretto, Titian, Tiepolo, and Canaletto among them. Their works are lodged
in a compound that includes the Scuola Grande di Santa Maria della Carità, the
Santa Maria church, and the Canonici Regolari Lateranensi monastery. The
museum is arranged chronologically in a counterclockwise manner.

DORSODURO

■ Byzantine and Gothic

Just beyond the entrance, Room 1 is dedicated to the earliest masters of the Venetian school. The distinctive style of this era—static religious figures on gold backdrops—reflects the Byzantine influence on the eastern Mediterranean that was only then starting to fade. Paolo Veneziano and Michele Giambono painted contrasting versions of the **"Coronation of the Virgin"** that hang in this room, while Lorenzo Veneziano rendered several of the 14th-century altarpieces. The room itself was once the main hall of the Scuola Grande di Santa Maria della Carità.

■ Renaissance

Nine different galleries (Rooms 2–10) display the museum's incredible Renaissance collection, which embraces many of the finest works produced in Venice at the time. Among the treasures of the first few rooms is Vittore Carpaccio's epic **"Crucifixion and Glorification of the Ten Thousand Martyrs of Mount Ararat,"** a graphic and rather gruesome image that mirrors the earlier work of Hieronymus Bosch. Other noteworthy paintings include a classic portrait of the Madonna and Child with John the Baptist by Giovanni Bellini,

"The Creation of the Animals" by Tintoretto, Andrea Mantegna's noble portrait of St. George (dead dragon at his feet), and a Titian version of John the Baptist. The Renaissance rises to a spectacular crescendo in Room 10 with two enormous paintings—**"Feast in the House of Levi"** by Paolo Veronese and **"The Miracle of St. Mark Freeing a Slave"** by Tintoretto. These colossal creations nearly overwhelm the moody **"Pietà,"** Titian's final work, which was apparently finished by Palma the Younger when the great master died in 1576. The painting also features a tiny self-portrait of Titian and his son kneeling in prayer, asking the Virgin Mary for delivery from the plague that would eventually take both their lives.

DORSODURO

One of several scenes from the legend of St. Ursula, by Vittore Carpaccio (1498)

■ BAROQUE AND ROCOCO

The Venetian obsession with religious themes continued well into the 16th and 17th centuries, as shown in the seven baroque galleries (Rooms 11–18). Among the master works of this section are **"The Translation of the Holy House of Loreto"** by Giambattista Tiepolo and **"Feast at the House of Simon"** by Bernardo Strozzi, a Genoa-born artist who often worked in Venice.

However, the faith-based works gradually give way to more secular themes that include landscapes, portraits of ordinary people, and portrayals of historic events. Among the best examples of these are Canaletto's meticulous urban landscapes and the lively genre scenes of Pietro Longhi, which show Venetian aristocrats getting fitted for new outfits, being dressed by their servants, and cavorting at balls.

The male domination of the art world was temporarily broken during this era, as shown by the works of Rosalba Carriera, a Venetian-born painter known for detailed miniature and pastel portraits of local aristocrats.

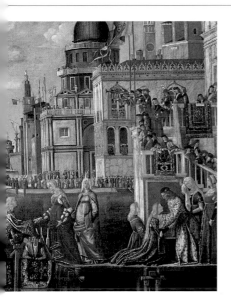

■ CYCLE PAINTINGS

The museum time-trips back to the Middle Ages in Rooms 20 and 21 for multipart artworks with specific themes. Several local masters including Gentile Bellini and Vittore Carpaccio contributed to **"Miracles of the Relic of the True Cross,"** an eight-part series originally commissioned for the Scuola Grande di San Giovanni Evangelista. Carpaccio's **"Healing of the Madman on the Rialto Bridge"** and Bellini's **"Procession in Piazza San Marco"** are the most renowned of these, both of them sprawling panoramas of life in Renaissance Venice. The other cycle is Carpaccio's epic nine-panel rendering of **"Scenes from the Legend of St. Ursula."** The series tells the story of the legendary Christian princess from Brittany who was captured by Attila the Hun and then martyred when she refused to marry him.

The old church of Santa Maria della Carità tenders additional Renaissance religious works while Room 24—which once served as the secretariat of the *scuola grande*—revolves around a triptych by Antonio Vivarini and Titian's **"Presentation of the Virgin at the Temple."** Painted in the 1530s, the latter is the only work in the entire museum displayed in its original location, a fitting end to a stroll through one of the world's greatest museums of fine art.

Tucked in among all the religious art is the sublime **"The Tempest"** by Giorgione, a mysterious painting of a nude woman, her child, and a male onlooker that the artist refused to explain during his lifetime. For more on Venetian artists, see pp. 144–147.

Campo della Carità 1050 • 041 520 0345 • €€€€ • Vaporetto: Accademia • gallerieaccademia.org

Venetian Artists

Surrounded by the soft, luminous light of the lagoon, and with a delight in color and surface textures inherited from Byzantium, painters working in Venice produced a distinctively Venetian art that reached its full expression during the Renaissance. They were also inspired by a love of the city itself, and much of their work can still be seen in the palaces and churches for which it was created.

Paolo Veneziano's "Madonna and Child"
Opposite: Gentile Bellini's "Procession in Piazza San Marco"

Byzantine Legacy

The first clearly identifiable painter in Venice is Paolo Veneziano (ca. 1300–1360). In 1345, he painted and signed the wooden cover of the Pala d'Oro (now in the **Museo di San Marco,** see p. 65), whose rich, deep colors, stylized figures, and decorative gold-leaf background are typically Byzantine.

The Bellini Family

The early Renaissance was dominated by the Bellini family, Jacopo and his two sons, Gentile and Giovanni. Most of Jacopo's (ca. 1400–1470) works have been destroyed, but two profoundly influential sketchbooks survive, with some 230 drawings of architecture, figures, and landscapes in which he experimented with linear perspective. Giovanni (ca. 1430–1516), the leading early Renaissance artist in Venice, adopted the new technique of oil painting in layers of transparent color. He became known for religious scenes in landscape settings bathed in atmospheric light and for his expressive use of color. He achieved a new sense of humanity in his figures, evident in several sublimely contemplative Madonnas in the **Gallerie dell'Accademia** (Academy Galleries; see pp. 140–143). Gentile (ca. 1429–1507) became a leading painter of *teleri,* narrative paintings of Venetian civic life, which the city's *scuole* commissioned for their headquarters. Like his "Procession in Piazza San Marco," painted in 1496 for the **Scuola Grande di San Marco** (see pp. 78–79), they usually included crowds of figures in architectural settings.

Masters of the High Renaissance

Perhaps the most brilliant artist to train in Bellini's studio was Giorgio da Castelfranco ("Giorgione"; ca. 1476–1510), who specialized in small paintings, mostly of secular subjects, produced for private collectors. They feature atmospheric landscapes in

which strange incidents and isolated figures appear, the best known being "The Tempest" in the **Gallerie dell'Accademia** (see p. 143).

Titian (1477–1576) was the first Venetian painter to gain an international reputation. In 1516, he was commissioned to paint the "The Assumption of the Virgin" for **Santa Maria Gloriosa dei Frari** (see pp. 120–121), whose size, scale, color, and realism quickly secured his reputation.

Titan's immediate successor was Jacopo Robusti (1519–1594), known as Tintoretto. Largely self-taught, Tintoretto earned commissions for Venetian churches, the scuole, and the **Palazzo Ducale** (Doge's Palace; see pp. 66–67). This prolific, passionate, and deeply religious artist produced works of high drama. The best place to see his work is the **Scuola Grande di San Rocco** (pp. 122–125).

Tintoretto's contemporary, Paolo Caliari (ca. 1528–88) from Verona, was known as Veronese. He produced ceiling paintings, feast scenes for the scuole, and altarpieces and quickly became one of the city's busiest artists. In contrast to those by Tintoretto, Veronese's paintings exuded relaxed enjoyment. Crowds of sumptuously dressed, aristocratic figures fill his vast canvases, which are also characterized by a skillful handling of space and luminous color.

Titian's "Assumption of the Virgin" (1516–1518)

DORSODURO

Veronese's "Rape of Europa," in the Palazzo Ducale

PORTRAITS OF VENICE

Rosalba Carriera (1675–1752) was particularly well known for her portraits in the new medium of pastels.

Pietro Longhi (1702–1785) painted popular scenes of patrician life.

Canaletto (Giovanni Antonio, 1697–1768) is famous for his *vedute,* views of Venice, from quiet squares to pageantry and festivals.

Francesco Guardi (1712–1793) specialized in vedute, favoring atmospheric effects over detail.

DORSODURO

Rococo Splendor

During the 17th century, painting went into a slight decline, but it flourished again in the 18th century. Giambattista (Giovanni Battista) Tiepolo (1696–1770), drawing inspiration from the work of Paolo Veronese, was the greatest fresco artist of the time. Often assisted by his son Gian Domenico, Tiepolo worked on decorative schemes and altarpieces all over the city of Venice. Among the finest examples of his swirling mythological scenes in clear bright colors twisting and swirling up into the heavens are those on view at the **Ca' Rezzonico** (see p. 138) and the **Scuola Grande dei Carmini** in Dorsoduro (*Dorsoduro 2616–2617, 041 528 9420, €€, scuolagrandecarmini.it*).

Venice's Campos

The city's neighborhood squares reveal a poetic sensibility that defies the monumental vibe of Piazza San Marco. The key to understanding domestic Venice—the gregarious interaction cherished by ordinary Venetians—is hanging out in some of the *campi* and watching everyday life swirl around you.

DORSODURO

■ Campo San Barnaba
It would be difficult to pinpoint a more picture-perfect Venetian square than the Campo San Barnaba in Dorsoduro—gondolas arrayed along the quay, old bridges leaping across the canal, a laid-back alfresco café, and the facade of a grand church looming above the cobblestones. The **Ponte dei Pugni** (Bridge of Fists) is where rival clans duked it out for many centuries. See if you can find the four marble footprints marking the starting point of these pugilistic rituals. Indiana Jones fans will recognize the square from *The Last Crusade*.

Fondamenta Gherardini 2771 • Vaporetto: Ca' Rezzonico

■ Campo Santa Maria Formosa
From a stone well and grand palaces to a busy gondola station, market stalls, and lovely Renaissance church, all of the iconic campo elements are present

in this Castello square, virtually untouched since Canaletto rendered the scene in the 1730s. Several of the hotels arrayed around the square occupy former aristocratic homes.

Calle del Mondo Novo • Vaporetto: Ospedale, Rialto, San Zaccaria

■ Campo della Bragora
Gothic is the vibe of this campo deep in the Castello district, a mood set by the 15th-century church of **San Giovanni in Bragora** (041 520 5906) and in the palaces arrayed around the square. Benches beneath the trees provide a shady rest to consider the facade of the Palazzo Gritti Badoer, and the Palazzo Soderini on the square's north side. **Caffè Girani** (041 721 500, €), a traditional Venetian hangout since 1928, roasts its own coffee beans.

Calle de la Pietà and Calle Terazzera • Vaporetto: San Zaccaria

A barge laden with fruit and vegetables trades alongside Campo San Barnaba in Dorsoduro.

■ CAMPO SAN GIACOMO DALL'ORIO
Wrapped around three sides of the
eponymous church (see p. 118), this
leafy square in Santa Croce attracts
local families and visitors seeking a
tranquil enclave, although its bars
and cafés do get busy after dark.

Campo San Giacomo dall'Orio • Vaporetto:
Riva de Biaisio

■ CAMPO SANTO STEFANO
By day, this San Marco campo is
bursting with tourists bustling
between nearby attractions; after dark
try its bars and boutiques. Buy

a gelato and perch yourself on the
steps below the statue of Italian
writer Niccolò Tommaseo.

Calle dello Spezier • Vaporetto: San
Samuele

■ CAMPO SAN POLO
This square (see pp. 118–119) is
renowned as the place where
Lorenzino de' Medici was felled by
two paid assassins in 1548. Nowadays
the square provides an airy venue for
Carnevale events (see pp. 126–127).

Salita San Polo • Vaporetto: San Tomà, San
Silvestro

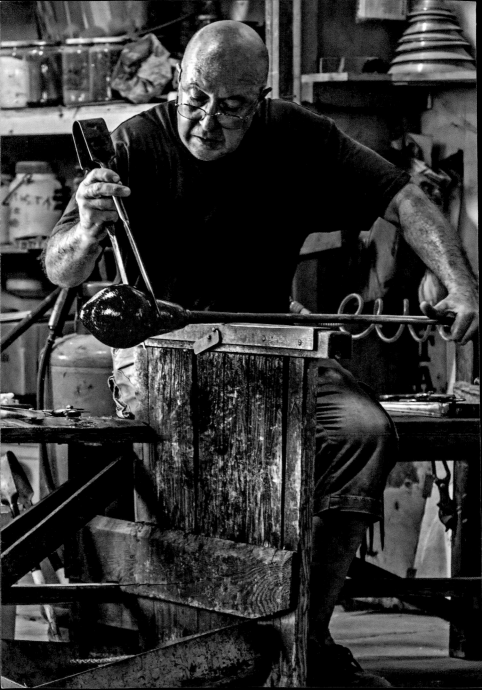

The Islands

Floating all around Venice is an archipelago of islands worthy of at least
a day's exploration. Reached by vaporetto or private boat, some of these
isles are home to communities that are even older than the city itself,
having been founded by those fleeing the mainland following the fall
of the Roman Empire. Once independent from Venice, many of these
islands flourished in their own right and continue to have an identity—
and even a regional accent—of their own today.

Although modern times have certainly reached
these shores, bygone ways and means persist in
the outer islands. Murano is still renowned for the
mastery of its glassblowers, Burano for its tradition
of skilled lacemaking, and Torcello for its
thousand-year-old churches with incredible
mosaics. But the lagoon offers much more than
history—it's also a great aquatic escape, a place
where Venetians and visitors alike get back to
nature on boats, bikes, beaches, and through
various other outdoor pursuits.

◀ **Glass has been made on
the island of Murano
since the Middle Ages.**

THE ISLANDS

The Islands

Ancient monuments and time-honored crafts are among the treasures that await visitors to Venice's outlying islands.

❶ Vetreria Artistica Vivarini (see p. 154) **After disembarking at the Colonna vaporetto dock, walk west along the waterfront to admire the craftsmanship at this cutting-edge glass atelier. Return to the dock and follow Fondamenta dei Vetrai across the island, cross Ponte Longo, and take Riva Longa and Fondamenta da Mula to the museum.**

❷ Museo del Vetro (see pp. 154–155) **See precious glassworks from ancient through modern times at this impressive collection. Turn left out of the museum and continue north on Fondamenta da Mula to Campo San Donato.**

❸ Basilica dei Santi Maria e Donato (see pp. 156–157) **Study the mysterious "dragon" bones and mosaics of this 12th-century church. Return to the Fondamenta da Mula, cross Campo Santo Stefano bridge, and make your way south to the Faro vaporetto pier. Hop on a vaporetto to Burano.**

SS14
CAMPALTO

0   3 kilometers
0   2 miles

L A G U N A
V E N E T A

MURANO

Basilica dei Santi Maria e Donato ❸

Museo del Vetro ❷

PONTE DELLA LIBERTÀ
SS11

Vetreria Artistica Vivarini ❶   Murano Museo

Murano V
Colonna   *SAN MICHELE*

VENEZIA (VENICE)

SAN GIORGIO IN ALGA

LA GIUDECCA

SAN GIORGIO MAGGIORE

SAN SERVOLO

LA GRAZIA

SAN CLEMENTE

SAN LAZZARO DEGLI ARMENI

LAZZARETTO VECCHIO

SACCA SESSOLA

SANTO SPIRITO

THE ISLANDS DISTANCE: APPROX. 12.5 MILES (20.2 KM)
TIME: APPROX. 8–10 HOURS VAPORETTO START: MURANO/COLONNA

THE ISLANDS

Palude
della
Rosa

Museo
di Torcello 7 5 Basilica di Santa
TORCELLO Maria Assunta
Torcello V 6
Chiesa di
Santa Fosca
Mazzorbo V V Burano
MAZZORBO 4 Burano
BURANO

MADONNA DEL MONTE

SAN GIACOMO
IN PALUDE

SANT'ERASMO

Litorale di S. Erasmo

PUNTA
SABBIONI

LE VIGNOLE

LA CERTOSA

SAN
NICOLÒ   Golfo di
LIDO DI   Venezia
VENEZIA
LIDO
Litorale di Lido

4 Burano
(see pp. 160–161)
Disembarking at the Mazzorbo or Burano docks, explore the Museo del Merletto, lace shops, and the rest of the island before catching another vaporetto to nearby Torcello island. From the Torcello pier, walk Fondamenta dei Borgognoni along the canal and toward the ancient church tower.

5 Basilica di Santa Maria Assunta
(see pp. 157–158) Renowned for its mosaics, this church is also the oldest building in Venice. On leaving, simply head next door.

7 Museo di Torcello (see p. 159)
Housed in two old palaces, this collection of lagoon artifacts varies from Paleolithic stone knives to Renaissance paintings.

6 Chiesa di Santa Fosca (see p. 158) Almost as old as Basilica di Santa Maria Assunta, this church contains the remains of two Catholic saints. Cross the grassy campo to the museum.

The normally mild-mannered island of Murano comes alive each year during the yuletide season, with a month-long celebration called the **Natale di Vetro** (Christmas of Glass), which starts on St. Nicholas Day *(Dec. 6)*. Past events have featured a **Tunnel of Lights** comprising chandeliers of Murano glass, a **Glassworks Regatta** between factory employees rowing traditional boats, and a **Furnace Food Festival** with dishes cooked in the glassworks' ovens.

Vetreria Artistica Vivarini

1 Glass reaches an artistic peak at this workshop, lodged behind a bloodred facade along the Murano waterfront. Founded in 1967, the Vivarini Glass Factory provides a space for local master glassmakers and visiting artists to create a wide variety of glass pieces, including sculptures, bowls, plates, vases, mirrors, candlesticks, glassware sets, and light fixtures. Many of the pieces are bespoke, created on commission from clients around the world. The glassmakers are given complete creative freedom, encouraged to experiment, and take the long tradition of Murano glass in new directions. Fred Wilson, Yoko Ono, Ben Vautier, Ugo Nespolo, and Armand Fernandez (a.k.a. Arman) are some of the artists who have forged pieces in the glass ovens at Vivarini.

Fondamenta Serenella 5/6, Murano • 041 736 077 • € • Vaporetto: Murano/Colonna • vivarini.it

Museo del Vetro

2 The story of glass from ancient through modern times is spun in this comprehensive collection at the Murano Glass Museum. Although the world's largest assemblage of Murano glass is undoubtedly the highlight, the museum flaunts an amazing array of pieces from various places and periods spanning 4,000 years of global glassmaking. Arranged chronologically, the collection kicks off with ancient pieces from Mesopotamia, Greece, and Rome before segueing into the Middle Ages and the golden age of Venetian glassmaking. Of special note are pieces by Murano glassmaker Angelo Barovier (1405–1460), who created the world's first clear or transparent glass and thereby revolutionized both the art form and the industry (see also pp. 162–163). There are also gorgeous works by 16th-century master Vincenzo d'Angelo dal

Gallo, decorated with lacelike diamond-point engraving. Other pieces showcase Murano innovations, such as iced glass, filigree, aventurine, and feather-shaped decoration, as well as a number of offbeat creations that include eccentric animal-shaped chandeliers and vases that were popular during the Renaissance.

The story continues with the decline of Venetian glass during the late 18th and early 19th centuries, when Bohemian glass became more popular. Discover how the glassmakers of Murano survived by mass-producing everyday glass objects rather than one-off works of art. The revival of Venetian glassmaking in the early 20th century is aptly reflected in the art nouveau bowls of Vittorio Toso Borella and the mosaic glass of Vittorio Zecchin. The final room presents works by modern masters, including Yoichi Ohira of Japan and American Dale Chihuly.

Fondamenta Giustinian 8, Murano • 041 739 586 • Closed Jan. 1, Dec. 25 • €€€
• Vaporetto: Murano Museo • museovetro.visitmuve.it

The Murano Glass Museum is housed in the island's former Palazzo Giustinian.

Basilica dei Santi Maria e Donato

3 Murano's paramount church is best known for mysterious bones and its floor rather than statues of saints or votive paintings. Erected in the 12th century on the site of several earlier churches, the Romanesque-style shrine honors both the Virgin Mary and Donatus of Arezzo, an early Christian saint who is said to have slain a dragon. Look for the four large bones hanging behind the main altar. According to legend, these are all that remain of the fiery reptile. Rather than dinosaur bones, it is more likely that these are Pleistocene fossils from some large mammal, perhaps a mammoth. Without doubt, the church's most outstanding aspect is the Byzantine-style mosaic floor with its geometric designs and wildlife portraits. You'll see peacocks, dragons, and a pair of chickens who appear to have captured a fox. The floor dates from around 1140, when the church was refashioned into its present form. Also

A large abacus with Murano glass beads stands before the Basilica dei Santa Maria e Donato.

worth noting are the golden glass mosaic of the Virgin Mary hovering above the apse and a stone sarcophagus that contains the bones of St. Donatus. The church exterior is plain by Venetian standards, a blend of red bricks and red tiles that reflect its Romanesque origins. The main facade faces west onto a cobblestone square, while the rounded eastern facade, with its white columns, rises above a canal. The campanile, separated from the church by a narrow walkway, towers to the south.

Campo San Donato, Murano • 041 739 056 • € • Vaporetto: Murano Museo • sandonatomurano.it

Burano

 (see pp. 160–161)

Laguna Veneto • Vaporetto: Burano, Mazzorbo

IN **THE KNOW**

Located just steps away from Torcello's medieval churches, **Locanda Cipriani** *(Piazza Santa Fosca 29, 041 730 150, €€€€)* offers classic Italian fare, fine wine, and plenty of history in a setting straight out of bygone Italy. Giuseppe Cipriani had already made a name for himself at **Harry's Bar** (see p. 17) when he took on the challenge of creating a country tavern in 1934. It immediately lured a hip crowd from Venice, including Ernest Hemingway who penned *Across the River and Through the Trees* while ensconced in a room above the restaurant. Other notable diners over the years include Winston Churchill, Marc Chagall, Maria Callas, and Diana, Princess of Wales.

Basilica di Santa Maria Assunta

Founded in 639, Torcello's ancient cathedral is a solid redbrick structure that was erected by mainlanders fleeing the wrath of Attila the Hun. Given numerous renovations over the years, little of that seventh-century church remains other than the outer walls of the nave and apse, and the ruined baptistery out front. Still, the overall style is a blend of the Byzantine and Romanesque influences that would come to define early Venetian architecture. After many years' use as a pigeon loft, the 11th-century campanile is now open to the public again, and it offers splendid views of Torcello and nearby isles. The interior is split into three naves divided by marble columns and separated from the apse by a lovely rood screen decorated with panels depicting flora and fauna. But the paramount reason for making the pilgrimage to this church—indeed the main reason for coming all the way out to

THE ISLANDS

Torcello—are the astonishing Byzantine-style mosaics, the earliest example of this ancient art form in all of Venice. Much of the floor comprises geometric tiles while an 11th-century **Madonna and Child** and their entourage of saints are poised above the apse. But none of this comes close to matching the brilliance of the **Last Judgment** mosaic on the west wall with its Dante-esque vision of hell. The Church of Santa Maria also safeguards relics of St. Heliodorus and St. Cecilia.

Piazza Torcello • €€ • Vaporetto: Torcello

GOOD **EATS**

■ ACQUASTANCA
A hip, modern design transformed this old bakery into a trendy Murano lunch spot. Fresh fish and pasta are complemented by wonderful homemade tiramisu and other desserts. **Fondamenta Manin 48, Murano, 041 319 5125, €€€**

■ AL CANTON
Tucked into a corner of Murano's Campo San Donato, this casual canalside café serves pasta and seafood combos like spaghetti with clams and grilled squid. **Campo San Donato 20, Murano, 041 527 5186, €€**

■ RIVA ROSA
Out-of-this-world risotto and seafood antipasto are just two of the delights at this family-run Burano eatery. Dine inside or on the rooftop terrace. **Via San Mauro 296, Burano, 041 730 850, €€€€**

Chiesa di Santa Fosca

6 Sharing the piazza with **Santa Maria Assunta** is another early Venetian church, this one dedicated to St. Fosca. Constructed during the 11th and 12th centuries, it seems even more Byzantine than its neighbor, built in the shape of a Greek rather than Latin cross and topped by a red-tiled dome. Looking at the facade, you'll see a marvelous portico comprising arches, white stone columns, and a bas relief of devotees kneeling before Fosca. The saint is buried within—you can see her remains inside a glass tomb beneath the altar. The 15-year-old Fosca was martyred along with her companion St. Maura around A.D. 250, when her father discovered her conversion to Christianity and turned her over to Roman authorities, who subsequently put them both to death. With its unadorned apse and wooden ceiling, Santa Fosca is even less embellished than Santa Maria Assunta.

Piazza Torcello • € • Vaporetto: Torcello

Museo di Torcello

7 Treasures from Torcello and nearby islands are on display in the small but interesting Torcello Museum on the opposite side of Piazza Torcello. The collection is split between two old buildings. The **Palazzo dell'Archivio** safeguards the archaeological relics, which range from Paleolithic stone axes to Etruscan pottery, Greek sculptures, Roman oil lamps, and an inkpot shaped like a stag. A brick wall hung with several dozen stelae connects the first building with the **Palazzo del Consiglio,** where the medieval and modern galleries cover the early Christian era through the 19th century. The artifacts run a broad gamut from Byzantine-style mosaics to Renaissance paintings. Among the more remarkable items are a 15th-century polychrome wood carving of St. Fosca's corpse, salvaged from the **Chiesa di Santa Fosca,** and a 13th-century gold-plated silver altarpiece.

Piazza Torcello • 041 730 761 • Closed Mon. • € • Vaporetto: Torcello • museoditorcello .provincia.venezia.it

This 15th-century marble relief depicting St. Bartholomew bearing his flesh hangs on a wall in the gardens at the Torcello Museum.

Burano

Burano is renowned for brightly painted houses, fresh seafood, and the incredibly intricate lacework created by buranelli *women.*

Exquisite garments on display in one of the many stores selling lace on the island.

This vibrant island town was founded in the sixth century A.D., but didn't thrive until the 16th century, when lacemaking became the island's hallmark. Meticulously rendered with needles rather than on a loom, Burano's *punto in aria* (stitch in air) technique took Europe by storm and made the island famous and wealthy. Local legend holds that the island's landmark colorful houses were born of an ancient custom of painting buildings in bright colors so fishermen could more easily identify their island in thick fog.

■ Museo del Merletto

Fine examples of the craft are on display at the Lace Museum (*Piazza Baldassare Galuppi 187, 041 730 034, €€*). The incredibly detailed designs on dresses, jackets, and linens rendered by Burano lacemakers during the Renaissance and baroque eras now grace the rooms in Podestà Palace, onetime home of the **Scuola dei Merletti** (Burano Lace School).

■ Embroidery Emporiums

Tablecloths, linens, and other embroidered items—as well as the occasional piece of antique lace—can be purchased at **La Perla Gallery** (*Via Galuppi 287 and 376, 041 730 009*) and other stores near Piazza Galuppi.

■ Leaning Tower

On the other side of the square is the **Chiesa di San Martino,** dedicated to the patron saint of Burano. The 15th-century church harbors a "crucifixion" by Giambattista Tiepolo, but is best known for its tilted campanile, slumped at an incline of 6 feet (1.83 m) in respect to its axis, and slowly sinking even farther into the soft island soil.

SAVVY **TRAVELER**

One of the quietest corners of the Venice lagoon is **San Francesco del Deserto Monastery** (*041 528 6863, closed Mon., entry by donation*) on the island of the same name. Founded in the 13th century after St. Francis of Assisi visited the island, the monastery is still tended by Franciscan monks in brown cassocks. Visitors are welcome, with monks leading tours around the grounds. The company LagunaFla (*041 528 6863, lagunaflaline.it*) runs private boats to the island from Burano.

■ Picture-Perfect

Most outlandish of the island's painted houses is **La Casa di Bepi Suà** (*Via al Gottolo 339*), a multicolored house covered in geometric designs and located on one of the narrow lanes off the Via Galuppi. Another colorful spot is the fishermen's wharf in front of the **Cooperativa San Marco,** where the local catch is landed each morning.

■ Mazzorbo

A footbridge leads to the adjoining island of **Mazzorbo,** a slice of rural life spangled with vegetable patches and tiny vineyards. The isle has its own small church, the **Chiesa di Santa Caterina** (*closed Tues.–Thurs.*), as well as Burano's cemetery.

THE ISLANDS

Laguna Veneta • Vaporetto: Burano, Mazzorbo

Venetian Crafts

With its pivotal position on East–West trade routes, the Venetian Republic had access to a continuous supply of valuable raw materials—silk, precious metals and gemstones, and rare pigments and dyes—from which the city's many artisans produced a wealth of luxury items. Although such industries operate on a tiny scale today, great craftsmanship remains central to Venetian life.

A 15th-century enameled glass from the Murano workshop
Opposite: An engraving depicting the doge visiting the Murano glass factory during the 17th century

Glass Perfection

Glassmaking probably began in Venice in Roman times. The city's glass furnaces moved to Murano during the 13th century, to reduce the risk of fire in Venice itself. Always innovating, Murano's glassmakers developed several new techniques. In the 15th century, Angelo Barovier discovered a way to make a clear, bubble-free glass. Known as *cristallo*, the method produced a thin, lightweight glass that was ideal for making elegant wineglasses. The glass known as *lattimo* also appeared during this time. Opaque and milky white in color, it imitated the highly popular Chinese porcelain being imported at the time. And, inspired by Ottoman glass, Murano's glassmakers used enameling and gilding for decorating goblets. Filigree—which involves weaving strands of lattimo or colored glass into a lattice or twisting them into spirals and setting them into clear glass—adorned bowls and glasses. New developments in the 17th century included *avventurina*, whereby flecks of metal were sprinkled into glass to create a shimmering effect.

Following a period of decline, the industry reemerged in the late 19th and 20th centuries, with firms such as Fratelli Toso, Salviati, and Venini joining old family glassmakers such as Barovier. New techniques included *sommerso,* produced by repeatedly dipping a piece of colored glass into a second color to produce a layered effect, and bubble-patterned *bullicante.* While some firms produce traditional items today—vases and bowls, glasses, mirrors, lamps, and figures—others commission international artists and designers to create contemporary art pieces. The "Vetro Artistico Murano" trademark distinguishes genuine Murano glass from the cheap imported imitations that fill many of Venice's shops.

Island Tradition

Just as Murano is famous for glass, nearby Burano is known for the quality of its handmade lace. Needlepoint laces, made with needle and thread, were first produced in Venice during the 16th century;

Venice gross point, which included padded stitching and has an embossed appearance, and the delicate rose point appeared in the 17th century on necklines and handkerchiefs. The first designs were geometric, but plants, flowers, and animals soon emerged. The very light Burano point appeared in the 18th century. By the end of the 16th century, bobbin laces were competing with needle laces. Nowadays, even on Burano, much of the lace on sale is machine-made, but it is possible to find handmade lace and to watch it being made by the few remaining lacemakers. Even a small piece can represent two months' work and prices are high.

Material Wealth

Venice is also known for its sumptuous fabrics. At the end of the 15th century, 2,000 looms were turning out soft velvets, lustrous damasks, and richly woven brocades shot through with silver or

Bobbin lacemaking on the island of Burano

Fortuny silk velvet fabric stamped in silver, 20th century

RARE
BOOKBINDING

The fusion of Eastern and Western ideas that runs through much Venetian design even influenced the craft of bookbinding. Printing was established in Venice in the 15th century. Venetian bookbinders mastered the Ottoman craft of binding books with leather and decorating them with hand-painted gold lettering and ornamentation. During the 18th century, they also adopted handmade marbled endpapers. A few binderies still exist, producing hand-printed papers and ranges of leather-bound journals, notebooks, and diaries.

gold thread. Early designs were Byzantine in origin, but Ottoman-inspired floral motifs also appeared. Today, the old skills are kept alive by a small number of companies. Probably the best known is Fortuny, founded by designer Mariano Fortuny in 1919, who devised a way of printing textiles by applying layers of color by hand. The Fortuny factory on Giudecca still produces furnishing fabrics in this way to Fortuny's original designs. Companies such as Bevilacqua and Rubelli draw on archives of traditional Renaissance patterns for some of their furnishing fabrics. They also weave some of their silk velvets and damasks on 17th- and 18th-century looms. The process produces a few hundred yards of fabric a year, and prices are correspondingly high. In addition, independent weavers produce silk, cotton, linen, and wool fabrics on handlooms for the fashion industry, as well as items such as shawls and scarves.

Summer on the Lagoon

The city's many waterways and islands provide the perfect combination for summer fun in Venice. Whether your ideal day is soaking up sun on a sandy shore or working up a healthy sweat on a bicycle, the lagoon offers dozens of ways to experience the great outdoors.

■ HIT THE BEACH

Between the islands of **Lido** and **Pellestrina** and the **Cavallino Peninsula,** Venice offers some 22 miles (35 km) of sand along the sparkling Adriatic Sea. The most celebrated (and crowded) stretch is Lido, which in 1857 became one of the world's first sea bathing resorts and a template for many other "lidos" around the globe. Nowadays, the celebrated strand offers public and private pockets of sand bedecked with colorful cabins, as well as cycling, scooter riding, and hiking along the Lungomare seafront and into the coastal sand dunes beyond.

■ CYCLE THE SHORE

With more than 200 bicycles in its fleet, **Venice Bike Rental** (*Granviale Santa Maria Elisabetta 79a, 041 526 1490, €–€€€, venicebikerental.com*) offers a central location between Lido's vaporetto pier and the main beach to hire a bike and take off. The Lungomare seafront is just up the block, marking the start of a 6.5-mile peddle (10.5 km) to the lagoon-side village of Malamocco and all the way down to Alberoni Beach at the south end of Lido island. In addition to 30-foot high sand dunes (9 m), Alberoni is where Luchino Visconti filmed much of Thomas Mann's *Death in Venice,* starring Dirk Bogarde, in 1971. Ambitious bikers can hop on a car ferry to adjacent Pellestrina island and cycle the 6.6-mile route (10.5 km) between Santa Maria del Mare and Villagio Ca' Roman—including a narrow portion surrounded by seawalls on both sides.

■ SCOOT AROUND

There's nothing quite as Italian as riding a scooter through the countryside . . . or along the Adriatic

Sailing on the island of Lido

coast. **Venice Scooter Rental** (*Via Negroponte 14, 388 888 8842, €€€€€, scooterrentvenice.com*) near the vaporetto pier in Lido has rentals ranging from two hours to seven days. The company also offers three-hour guided scooter tours of Lido and Pellestrina islands between April and September for those who don't want to explore on their own. The scooter routes across these islands are similar to the cycle routes listed above, although the narrow southern extreme of Pellestrina is too rugged for vehicular traffic.

■ WINE AND DINE LIKE A STAR
Follow in the footsteps of many a celebrity and dine at **Ristorante Tropicana** (*Lungomare Guglielmo Marconi 41, 041 526 0201, €€€€€, hotelexcelsiorvenezia.com*), a time warp for Mediterranean cuisine overlooking the Adriatic shore of Lido island. Located in the Moorish-style **Hotel Excelsior,** it is a traditional haunt of actors, directors, and other luminaries attending the **Venice Film Festival** (see pp. 168–169). During the colder months of the year, meals are taken indoors beneath chandeliers and a

Movie fans wait for an autograph-signing event in front of the Palazzo del Cinema, Lido island.

wooden beamed ceiling. But during the summer, the action moves onto the outdoor terrace with its candlelit tables overlooking the sea. Also popular with the silver-screen crowd is **La Tavernetta** *(Via Francesco Morosini 4, 041 526 1417, €€€€, latavernettalido.com)*, where the menu combines Venetian seafood and Tuscan meat dishes with some 150 different Italian wines. The ambience is homey and the walls are lavishly decorated with framed photographs of the many celluloid legends who have dined there.

■ Catch a Flick

Founded in 1932, and one of the world's most prestigious cinematic events of the year, the **Venice Film Festival** takes up residence on Lido at the end of every summer. The 11-day festival kicks off in late August and spills over into early September. Its main venue is the **Palazzo del Cinema** *(Lungomare Guglielmo Marconi, 041 521 8711)* near the south end of the main beach. The art deco movie palace houses three screening rooms including an 1,100-seat main theater, idolized by moviemakers around the world. Federico Fellini once quipped that "entering the Palazzo del Cinema at the Venice Film Festival was like passing a final exam." The movie lineup for the upcoming festival is normally announced in July.

■ Row a Boat

Locals have been propelling themselves across the lagoons with poles and oars for more than 2,000 years. So why not visitors, too? Based in Cannaregio, **Row Venice** (*345 241 5266, €€€€€, rowvenice.org*) offers hands-on instruction in the *voga alla veneta*—the Venetian style of rowing while standing up and facing forward à la gondolier. Run almost entirely by women, the nonprofit educational organization is dedicated to the preservation and promotion of traditional Venetian water culture. Lessons last about 90 minutes and take place on both quiet side canals and the open lagoon in a traditional wooden *batelina*. Children are welcome and instruction is available in six different languages including English. *Vogata di Sera* evening rowing sessions on the Grand Canal are also offered, as well as a *Cicchetto Row* that combines rowing with a light evening meal.

■ Paddle the Lagoon

The warren of waterways that surround Venice is ideal for a kayaking experience that combines a historic urban environment and the wide open spaces of a large Adriatic lagoon. From its beach base on the island of La Certosa, **Venice Kayak** (*346 477 1327, €€€€€, venicekayak.com*) offers a variety of half- and full-day tours that cruise the Grand Canal, St. Mark's Basin, and smaller waterways. Day trips around Burano, Torcello, San Francesco del Deserto, and La Certosa islands, and local salt marshes are also available. The company also has history and after-dark itineraries, both group and private tours, and bespoke paddle tours set around special events. Children eight and over are welcome and all guides speak English.

IN **THE KNOW**

With two itineraries on offer, **Terra e Acqua** (347 420 5004, €€€€, veniceboat .org) operates daylong boat tours of the lagoon. The traditional, wooden *bragosso* boats accept groups of 9–12 people. Depending on the itinerary you choose (North or South Lagoon), you will have the chance to meet local fishermen, to visit an ancient monastery on the Island of San Lazzaro degli Armeni, and to shop for baby artichokes on the Island of Sant'Erasmo. Best of all, you'll experience all the beauty of this natural habitat at close hand.

PART 3

Travel Essentials

PLANNING YOUR TRIP

When to Go

Venice is beautiful year-round and there are certain advantages to be had from both peak-time and off-peak visits.

In the **winter** months, a magical mist descends upon Venice giving the city a romantic air. You are also more likely to see an *acqua alta* at this time of year. Literally translating as "high water," this is when the lagoon rises owing to tidal peaks in the Adriatic Sea, and parts of the city flood. Winter also brings the benefits that come with attracting fewer tourists, allowing visitors to explore and navigate the city with a lot more ease and grace than is possible in summertime. An important festival takes place during winter—the **Festa della Madonna della Salute** *(Nov. 21).*

The disadvantages of visiting Venice during the winter months is that a number of museums have shorter hours, and some businesses close completely for **January/ February,** then reopen only when **Carnevale** comes around *(usually between February and March, lasting for ten days prior to Lent):* It is one of the most important events in Venice.

The season in which everything is sure to be open is from **April to October,** with the exception of the month of **August,** when, like most Italians, the Venetians themselves go on vacation.

A huge plus during the summer months, is that you can eat and drink alfresco, enjoying the many opportunities to dine by the edge of the lagoon, beside any number of winding canals, or in one of the many campos dotted throughout the city. You can also visit **Lido** and hire a bike from **Venice Bike Rental** *(Granviale Santa Maria Elisabetta 79a, 041 526 1490, €–€€€, venicebikerental.com).*

In **June** every year, the **Biennale di Venezia** opens, alternating between the arts one year and architecture the next. **Art Night Venezia** *(June 21)* celebrates an evening of culture, during which some 100 museums and art galleries stay open until around midnight and there are many live performances and art and music events.

In **July,** visitors can see local events that include the **Festa del Redentore** and the **Festa di San Giacomo dall'Orio,** and in **September,** the **Venice Film Festival** and the **Regata Storica.**

Climate

Venice is pretty mild by global standards, but temperatures fluctuate. Check the forecast in the week before your stay, and you will notice that the predicted weather will change about 10 times before you actually arrive!

The winters are cold, but temperatures rarely drop below 30°F (–1°C). A few nights reach 26.5°F (–3°C), but these are an exception and the majority of the time the temperature

stays between 32 and 50°F (0°–10°C). Snow is rare—a light dusting disappearing almost as quickly as it falls.

November can be the grimmest of months, as this is also traditionally the wettest. With the rainfall, the likelihood of an acqua alta occurring increases, and the city feels bleaker than at any other time of the year. This is especially the case if the city is damp or foggy, both of which make the place feel more chilly.

December and **January** can be cold but there is a greater chance of the sky being crisp and blue, while **February** might see a return of acqua alta. Temperatures between **February** and **March** generally fluctuate from as low as 41°F to as high as 57°F (5°–14°C).

Once **April** arrives the temperature reaches 60°F+ (15.5°C+) and the possibility of blue skies are greatly increased. **May** and **June** are beautiful— the latter with highs above 85°F (29.5°C) in recent years.

July and **August** are usually the hottest months with temperatures ranging from 80 to 92°F (26.5°–33°C). These months can also be very humid, especially in the city itself, so many locals take advantage of Lido nearby and rent a beach hut for the entire season. **September** is a very pleasant month—warm, but without the sticky humidity of high summer—and with sunny days stretching into early **October.**

For optimum sightseeing weather, plan your trip for either **May** or **September.**

These months are neither too hot, nor too humid, nor too cold. They also tend to experience the least rainfall.

What to Take

Venice is reliant on tourism and, as in all European cities, you can generally get whatever you need nowadays.

If there is any chance of an acqua alta during your visit, you will definitely need galoshes, an umbrella, and plastic protective gear. However, since most airlines have baggage limits, you might prefer to buy these on arrival— they are all readily available— and save your luggage weight for more important things.

There are many pharmacies in Venice. It is worth noting that many drugs requiring prescriptions in other countries may be bought over the counter in Italy. Nevertheless, if you have prescription drugs of your own, you should still bring them, in case they are not available.

Passports

U.S. and Canadian citizens can stay in Italy for up to three months with just a valid passport. No visa is required. Passports should be valid for at least six months beyond your departure date. It is always best to check the details of this with your consulate (see p. 177) before traveling.

Insurance

It is always advisable to take out travel insurance in the event that anything happens to you while you are abroad. This is especially true in the case of theft, repatriation, travel cancellations, and delays.

If major credit cards have been used to pay for flights and accommodations, your credit card company may also cover certain losses.

Most travelers from outside the EU will need insurance coverage for any nonmedical emergencies and aftercare treatment.

Theft & Loss

In the case of theft, you need to head to the central police station in **Piazza San Marco** to make an official police report. There are translators on hand for most foreign languages. If you intend to make an insurance claim, or need to apply for a new passport, it is essential that you have a copy of this report.

Medical

In the case of an accident, everyone in Italy is entitled to free emergency services For further help or aftercare, European citizens are covered, free of charge, under the **European Health Insurance** card. Other nations should check to see if they have a reciprocal agreement with Italy for public health care access.

Travelers outside of the EU should make sure they have adequate medical coverage to cover any expenses that fall outside of what would be considered emergency medical treatment.

Further Reading

There are many great books to read in order to gain a greater insight and feel for Venice:

Fiction
- *Death in Venice,* Thomas Mann
- *The Aspern Papers,* Henry James
- *The Comfort of Strangers,* Ian McEwan
- *Don't Look Now,* Daphne du Maurier
- *Dead Lagoon,* Michael Dibdin
- *A Thousand Days in Venice,* Marlena de Blasi
- The Commissario Guido Brunetti crime novels, Donna Leon

Nonfiction
- *A Venetian Affair,* Andrea di Robilant
- *Francesco's Venice,* Francesco da Mosto
- *The Secrets of the Grand Canal: Mysteries, Anecdotes, Curiosities About the Most Beautiful Boulevard in the World,* Toso Fei
- *Venice: History of the Floating City,* Joanne M. Ferraro

HOW TO GET TO VENICE

By Air

Venice can be accessed by two major airports, **Marco Polo,** the city's main terminal, and **Treviso,** at which Ryanair has its Venice base. Marco Polo airport is a 35-minute bus ride from the city center, and you can buy tickets at the **HelloVenezia** (*veneziaunica.it*) desk inside the airport or look for a ticket machine near the bus stop. **AeroBus No. 5** (*041 240 1701, 8€, actv.it*) drives directly to Piazzale Roma. From there you can catch a vaporetto to major destinations in the city.

Alternatively, if you take the 10-minute walk to the lagoon waterfront (left on exiting the airport), you can catch an **Alilaguna** (*041 240 1701, 15€ one way, alilaguna.it*) boat. The service offers four different color-coded lines, and covers various routes and stops in Venice and on the islands of Lido and Murano. All travel details can be found, in English, on the website so it is very easy to plan your route depending on where you are staying.

You can also reach the city by taking a **water taxi**—expect to pay 80–120€—or a taxi cab by land to Piazzale Roma for around 60€.

Reaching Venice from Treviso airport is very straightforward; buy a ticket on your plane and catch an **Atvo Bus** (*12€ one way, atvo.it*) directly outside the airport. The journey takes around 40 minutes.

By Train
Venice has been connected by train to mainland Italy since the 1860s. The city's main train station, **Stazione Venezia Santa Lucia** (*grandistazioni .it*), is at the foot of the Grand Canal, just behind the Ferrovia vaporetto station. It links Venice with all major cities in Italy as well as many cities in

mainland Europe, including Paris, Vienna, and Munich.

By Car
Arriving in Venice by car, you will come directly into Piazzale Roma and can go no farther, as Venice is an entirely car-free city. There are many options for parking. At Piazzale Roma, **Garage San Marco** (*Piazzale Roma 467/F, 041 523 2213, garagesanmarco.it*) has 900 spaces and a flat rate of 30€ for 24 hours.

Another option is to park at Tronchetto to the west of the city, where **Venezia Tronchetto Parking** (*Isola Nuova del Tronchetto, 041 520 7555, veniceparking.it*) has some 4,000 spaces and a rate of 21€ for 24 hours. There are easy transportation links from Tronchetto to central Venice.

By Bus
Eurolines (*0861 1991900, eurolines.it*), **GoEuro** (*goeuro .com*), and **FlixBus** (*+49 030 300 137 300, flixbus.it*), all operate services to Venice from other major Italian cities and/ or from many European cities. As an example, the journey from Genoa to Venice takes 5 hours 50 minutes and costs 15€—half the price of the same journey by train, and only one hour longer.

GETTING AROUND

Public Transportation
In Venice, the primary public transportation system runs on the water, either by vaporetto,

motoscafo, or *motonave,* all operated by **ACTV** (*actv .avmspa.it*). The most common of these, the **vaporettos** are the flat-decked vessels that operate on the main city routes on and around the Grand Canal. **Motoscafi** are more streamlined and better protected from the elements. These operate on routes that travel outside the sheltered waters of the Grand Canal, the Giudecca Canal, and St. Mark's Basin. Routes to the islands of Murano, Burano, Torcello, and Lido are operated by **motonave,** the largest of the waterbuses.

Waterbus routes sometimes change and a number of them are seasonal. For the most reliable guide, download a printable route map from the ACTV website just before you head off to Venice.

Also, within the city, you will also see *traghetto* (ferry) points from which you can hop across the canal in a larger version of a gondola rowed by two gondoliers. This service operates daily from 7 a.m. to 7 p.m. (*2€, paid directly to the gondolier*).

Buying Tickets
Most of the larger vaporetto stations—Rialto, San Marco-Vallaresso, and San Zaccaria, for example—have an **ACTV or HelloVenezia** ticket (*biglietto*) office. Failing that, and at smaller vaporetto stops, there are ACTV touch-screen ticket-vending machines. The price (*7.50€ one-way fare, valid for 75 minutes*) is the same no matter

which vessel you use. All tickets must be stamped in a ticket-validating machine prior to use. **Tourist Travel Cards** are available for one, two, three, or seven days *(20€, 30€, 40€, 60€, respectively)*. These passes allow you to hop on and off the waterbuses as much as you like.

Water Taxis
Consorzio Motoscafi Venezia *(041 522 2303, motoscafivenezia.it)* operates a water taxi service. A taxi from the airport to your hotel will cost 100€—a standard price covering up to five passengers with five pieces of luggage. Extra people are charged at 10€ per person. Your hotel will be able to book a taxi for you or you can make a booking online.

Gondolas
The romantic way to travel is by gondola, with stations located at **Bacino Orseolo** (see p. 60) and on the Grand Canal at **Rialto.** You'll also find a gondolier or two sitting beside a bridge in most of the larger campos. The price is 80€ for 30 minutes, for a maximum of six people. Nighttime rides cost 100€ for 35 minutes.

On Foot
Despite Venice being very small, it is possible to spend hours getting lost. But there is a certain charm in following narrow winding streets and bridges. Allow yourself to explore and see where each turn takes you—often pretty little squares unfold in front of you quite by surprise.

If you need to be somewhere and are short of time, make sure you have a good map with you—in fact, you should always carry a map. Ask your hotel reception for one—they usually give them out free of charge.

To walk from one side of Venice to the other takes just over one hour at a leisurely pace. There is a system of signs to help orient you to main areas within the city—for example, the train station, the Piazza San Marco and Rialto areas, and Piazzale Roma.

PRACTICAL ADVICE

National Holidays
In Venice, museums are open on holidays except for Jan. 1 and Dec. 25. The main Bank Holidays in Venice are:

- **January 1** (New Year's Day)
- **January 6** (Epiphany)
- **Easter Monday**
- **April 25** (Liberation Day; Feast of St. Mark)
- **May 1** (Labor Day)
- **June 2** (Republic Day)
- **August 15** (Assumption)
- **November 1** (All Saint's Day)
- **December 8** (Immaculate Conception)
- **December 25** (Christmas Day)
- **December 26** (St. Stephen's Day)

Money
Venice is in the euro zone so only euros are accepted throughout the city. Most

shops, bars, and restaurants take credit cards and debit cards without any problems and there are many ATMs dotted around the city. There are currency exchange shops at **Piazzale Roma, Rialto,** and **San Marco.**

Banks in Venice are mainly concentrated to the west of Piazza San Marco. Opening hours are usually Mon.–Fri., 8:30 a.m.–1:30 p.m. and 2:30 p.m.–3:30 p.m.

Opening Times
Opening times in Venice are generally 9 a.m.–7 p.m., but these times vary, with some shops opening at 8 a.m. and some closing at 7.30 p.m. Large department stores, retail chains, cell phone stores, and tourist-oriented shops will stay open all day, while some smaller shops and pharmacies close from 12:30 p.m.–3:30 p.m.

Post Offices
There are eight post offices in Venice. Their opening times vary but all of them open at 8:20 a.m., some of the smaller offices close at 1:35 p.m., but the larger branches stay open until 7:05 p.m. The three main post offices are located at the following places:

- **San Marco** *(Calle Larga de l'Ascension 1241, 041 244 6711)*
- **Rialto** *(Calle de le Acque 5016, 041 240 4149)*
- **Piazzale Roma** *(Fondamenta Santa Chiara, Santa Croce 511, 041 244 6811).*

Places of Worship

Venice has a Roman Catholic church in every parish so you don't have to walk very far to find the next place of worship. Many operate services, but most are also tourist attractions. They post their service times on the front door and these vary from church to church. **St. George's Anglican Church** *(Campo San Vio, Dorsoduro)* offers a Sunday service in English *(10:30 a.m.)*.

Venice has a very active and lively Jewish quarter in the Cannaregio neighborhood, where there are also five main synagogues. All details about celebrations and weekly gatherings can be found on *jewishvenice.org*.

Museum Cards

In recent years, Venice has developed an all-in-one city pass called **Venezia Unica** *(veneziaunica.it)*. Tourists can go online and create and customize their own passes. The beauty of Venezia Unica is that you can also include other services on this card. In addition to the city's key sights, you can add transport, Wi-Fi access, a toilet pass, and various other services. A pass with everything included costs 136,90€, and includes airport transfers.

If you are just interested in seeing the main museums, the **Museum Pass** *(24€, venice -museum.com)* is excellent value and gives access to the following sights: **Palazzo Ducale** (Doge's Palace; see pp. 66–67); **Museo Correr** (Correr Museum; see

p. 60); **Museo Archeologico Nazionale** (Archaeological Museum; *Piazzetta San Marco 17, 041 522 5978, archeoveneto .it*); **Biblioteca Nazionale Marciana** (St. Mark's Library; see p. 60); **Ca' Rezzonico** (see p. 138); **Palazzo Mocenigo** (see p. 117); **House of Carlo Goldoni** *(San Polo 2794, 041 275 9325, closed Wed., carlogoldoni.visitmuve.it)*; **Ca' Pesaro** (see pp. 116–117); **Museo del Vetro** (Murano Glass Museum; see pp. 154–155); **Museo del Merletto** (Burano Lace Museum; see p. 161); and **Fondaco dei Turchi** (Natural History Museum; see p. 49).

Entry to most churches in Venice costs 3€. Buying a **Chorus Pass** *(041 275 0462, chorusvenezia.org)*, gives free entry to 18 churches throughout the city. You can purchase your ticket from the website in advance of traveling, or buy it at any of the participating venues: Chiesa di Santa Maria del Giglio; Chiesa di Santo Stefano; Chiesa di Santa Maria Formosa; Chiesa di Santa Maria dei Miracoli; Chiesa di San Giovanni; Elemosinario; **Chiesa di San Polo** (see p. 119); **Basilica di Santa Maria Gloriosa dei Frari** (see pp. 120–121); **Chiesa di San Giacomo dall'Orio** (see p. 118); Chiesa di San Stae; Chiesa di Sant'Alvise; Basilica di San Pietro di Castello; **Chiesa del Santissimo Redentore** (see p. 135); **Chiesa di Santa Maria del Rosario** (I Gesuati; see p. 137); Chiesa di San Sebastiano; Chiesa di San Giobbe; Chiesa di San

Giuseppe di Castello; Chiesa di San Vidal; and Chiesa di San Giacomo di Rialto.

Restrooms

Venice is not a very restroom friendly city. Most bars and restaurants will not let you use their facilities unless you buy a coffee or a drink first. If you don't want to do this, there are 11 public toilets spread around the city. The opening times vary. For example: **Venezia Santa Lucia Station** *(6 a.m.– 11 p.m.)*; **Rialto** *(7 a.m.–7 p.m.)*; and **San Marco** *(9 a.m.–8 p.m.)*. The cost is 80 cents.

Safety

Venice is a very safe city, even at night. Pickpocketing has been known during the day in busy tourist areas, so be aware of your belongings if you find yourself in a large crowd, on a vaporetto, or around San Marco and the Rialto. Throngs of tourists make easy targets while busy seeing the sights and taking photographs

In recent years there has been a rise in the number of burglaries during the summer months, from first- and second-floor apartments. If you are renting an apartment on either of these floors, close your windows and shutters when you go out, and at night.

Telephones

Most people have their cell phones while traveling, but if you are planning on being in Italy for a few weeks it might be worth picking up an Italian SIM card to use while you are there.

You will need your passport to buy one. The main providers are **TIM, Vodafone,** and **Wind.** There are also public telephones dotted around the city, which accept coins or cards, and phone cards can be bought at a *tabaccaio,* which is a shop that sells cigarettes.

Time Differences

Venice is on central European time (CET)—one hour ahead of London, and usually six hours ahead of New York and nine hours ahead of Los Angeles. It is also six hours behind Beijing, eight behind Sydney, and ten behind Auckland. Italy participates in daylight saving time, with the clocks going forward in March and backward in October. There are 2–3 weeks in spring and fall when the United States have changed their clocks but Europe hasn't.

Tipping

In general, restaurants include a service charge so tips are not expected. Obviously, if you are happy with the service, leaving a tip is at your discretion.

Travelers With Disabilities

Although facilities have improved for disabled visitors in recent years, Venice remains a very difficult city to navigate in a wheelchair. Most of the inner-city bridges lack ramps. You will find ramps along the Zattere and from San Marco to Saint Elena, however. The best way to navigate the city by wheelchair is by vaporetto; the ACTV staff are very used to helping disabled passengers on and off boats.

Around 70 percent of the city can be accessed by vaporetto; a very detailed map can be found on the **City of Venezia** website *(comune.venezia.it).*

Visitor Information

There are seven **Tourist Information offices** *(041 529 8711, turismovenezia.it)* in and around Venice. The main offices are:
- **San Marco Airport** *(Aeroporto Marco Polo, 30030)*
- **San Marco** *(71/f, San Marco)*
- **Piazzale Roma** *(Piazzale Roma Garage ASM)*
- **Venezia Santa Lucia Station** *(Stazione Ferroviaria Santa Lucia)*

EMERGENCIES

Embassies
- **U.S. Consular Agency** *(Viale Galileo Galilei 30, 041 541 6654)*
- **Canadian Consulate** *(Piazza Cavour 3, Milan, 02 6269 4238)*
- **British Consulate** *(Piazzale Donatori di Sangue 2/5, 041 505 5990)*

Phone Numbers
- **Police** *112*
- **Fire brigade** *115*
- **Ambulance** *118*

Health
The city is very well equipped to deal with emergencies. There is a first-aid office at **San Marco** *(Piazza San Marco 63/65, Procuratie Nuove)* and an office at **Piazzale Roma** *(Santa Croce 496, Piazzale Roma).* These two points are walk-in centers. Consult the website

healthvenice.com for more information. If you require a doctor after hours, contact:
- **Centro Storico Venezia** (historic center; 041 529 4060)
- **Mestre Sud, Marghera,** and **Mestre Nord** *(041 965 7999).*
  Pharmacies are open from 8.30–12.30 a.m. and 3.30–7.30 p.m. *(Mon.–Fri.),* and 8.30–12.30 a.m. *(Sat.).* They are usually closed on Sundays, although there is a night rota system in Venice so there is always one pharmacy on call *(farmacistivenezia.it).*

  In case of an emergency, or if you accidentally fall into the canal, call *118* for an ambulance. The hospital is located in Castello: **Ospedale Santi Giovanni e Paolo** *(Fondamenta Nuove, Castello 6777, 041 529 4111).*

Lost Property
Venice's Lost Property Office, **Ufficio Oggetti Rinvenuti** *(San Marco 4136, 041 274 8225),* is located at Rialto on the San Marco side of the Grand Canal. Other useful offices:
- **Office of the Traffic Police** *(Piazzale Roma, 041 522 4576/270 8225)*
- **ACTV Vaporetti Lost Property** *(Cannaregio 3935, 041 272 2179)*
- **ACTV Bus Lost Property** *(Galleria Teatro Vecchio, 041 272 2838)*
- **Airport Lost Property** *(041 260 9222/260 6436)*
- **Venezia Santa Lucia Station** *(Stazione Ferroviaria Santa Lucia, 041 785 531)*

HOTELS

Venice is hugely geared toward tourism and has accommodations to suit all requirements and budgets. Those looking for the convenience of a hotel will find everything from a luxury palazzo oozing 18th-century opulence and luxury to an equally comfortable contemporary boutique. With the boom of **airbnb,** there are also thousands of apartments to hire, giving you greater flexibility and, potentially, a more economical stay in the city.

TRAVEL ESSENTIALS

Venice has hundreds of hotels and it's a good idea to consider all the options before choosing where you want to stay. Take both your interests and your needs into account when selecting an area of the city to stay in. Also think about the timing of your visit. At certain times of the year—during Carnevale or the Biennale di Venezia, for example—rooms are at a premium. You'll need to book well in advance to avoid excessive rates and/or disappointment.

Before making a booking be sure to double-check the address. Some hotels advertised as being in Venice are actually based in Mestre. While this has its advantages—room prices are lower in Mestre and it is easy to get to Venice by bus—it would be a shame to book a hotel there in error. Look for the word "via" in the address, as this means it is in Mestre.

Those staying in Venice itself will find it very quiet, as there is no noise from traffic. Having said that, rooms with canal views can be noisy early in the morning with deliveries by barge, rubbish collection boats, and trolleys. Conversely, rooms overlooking any of the campos can be noisy at nighttime if bars

and restaurants have alfresco seating. In general, all bars and restaurants close by 11:30 p.m. or 12 a.m., with the exception of Campo Santa Margherita where some bars stay open until at least 3 a.m.

Hotel prices generally include all taxes and charges, Wi-Fi, and a continental breakfast. Many online sites offer bargains, so that's a good place to start. If you are planning on staying longer than a week, an apartment can work out to be much more reasonable. Apartment rental is big business in Venice, with many apartments available for rent to tourists through travel agents. If you are planning on a longer stay during the summer months, staying on the island of Lido is an excellent option, as there are beaches and plenty of nightlife. Then it is just a short boat ride across to Venice for sightseeing.

Organization

The hotels listed on the following pages have been grouped according to their neighborhood, from San Marco to the Islands. Within each group, accommodations are then listed alphabetically by price range.

Price Range

The prices given are for double rooms in the high season and the price range is indicated in euros.

€€€€€	More than €300
€€€€	€180–€300
€€€	€80–€180
€€	€50–€80
€	Less than €50

Text Symbols

(**i**) No. of Guest Rooms
Vaporetto Elevator
Air-conditioning Wi-Fi
Nonsmoking Outdoor Pool
Health Club/Gym/Spa
Credit Cards

SAN MARCO

With the city's highest concentration of exclusive hotels and resorts, San Marco is the *sestiere* for high-end luxury. There are also many restaurants and boutique shops in this area, as well as some of the city's major sights. You will be in close proximity to the **Palazzo Ducale** (Doge's Palace; see pp. 66–67), the **Basilica di San Marco** (St. Mark's Basilica (see pp. 64–65), and the opulent **Piazza San Marco** (St. Mark's Square; see pp. 58–59). If there is a downside, San Marco can get incredibly busy, especially in summer. But if you don't mind the crowds and you want to be in the heart of things, this is the place to be. This location is great for boat access.

■ BAGLIONI HOTEL LUNA
€€€€€
SAN MARCO 1243
TEL 041 528 9840
baglionihotels.com
The Baglioni Hotel Luna has a fantastic location right next to Piazza San Marco and is one of the many stunning five-star hotels in this exclusive area. It has many wonderful Venetian furnishings, a beautiful rooftop terrace, and an excellent record for service and satisfaction.
ⓘ *68, plus 36 suites*
🚤 *San Marco* 🔄 🛗 🛜 🅾️
🅰️ *All major cards*

■ THE BAUER VENEZIA
€€€€€
SAN MARCO 1459
TEL 041 520 7022
bauervenezia.com
The Bauer complex offers many stunning options for a stay in Venice, set across four beautiful palazzos. The rooms are exquisite, charming, and luxurious—full of 15th-century style. The most private experience is Casa Nova, where the well-equipped apartments are ideal for a longer stay. Located near Piazza San Marco, the hotel is also close to several vaporetto stops.
ⓘ *107, plus 31 suites*
🚤 *San Marco* 🔄 🛗 🛜 🅾️
🅰️ *All major cards*

■ THE GRITTI PALACE
€€€€€
CAMPO SANTA MARIA DEL GIGLIO 2467
TEL 041 794 611
thegrittipalace.com
Once a palace belonging to one of Venice's greatest merchant families, The Gritti Palace remains one of the city's finest hotels. The rooms are large and have all the characteristic Venetian decor you would expect to find in a hotel of this standard. Ernest Hemingway loved to stay here. The terrace offers exquisite views of the Chiesa di Santa Maria della Salute and the Grand Canal.
ⓘ *82, plus 21 suites*
🚤 *Santa Maria del Giglio*
🔄 🛗 🛜 🅾️ 🍽️
🅰️ *All major cards*

■ PALAZZINA G
€€€€€
RAMO GRASSI 3247
TEL 041 528 4644
palazzinag.com
The Palazzina G offers six types of rooms and apartment suites—all in five-star luxury and with a modern-style design by Philippe Starck. A number of rooms overlook the Grand Canal, and the hotel's fabulous bar and restaurant only add to the exclusive experience of staying here.
ⓘ *22* 🚤 *San Samuele*
🔄 🛗 🅾️
🅰️ *All major cards*

■ NH COLLECTION PALAZZO BAROCCI
€€€€€
CORTE DELL'ALBERO 3878/A, 30124

TEL 041 296 0650
nh-collection.com
This comfortable hotel was built in 1890 and was once a theater in which Vivaldi made regular musical appearances. Rooms are contemporary in design—some with views of the Grand Canal—and the junior suites have a bath in the middle of the bedroom. Among the highlights is the hotel's secluded landscaped garden, complete with fountain—the perfect place to relax after a long day exploring.
ⓘ *59, including a number of suites*
🚤 *Sant'Angelo* 🔄 🛗 🛜 🅾️
🅰️ *All major cards*

■ CORTE DI GABRIELA
€€€€€
CALLE DEGLI AVVOCATI 3836
TEL 041 523 5077
cortedigabriela.com
This luxurious hotel has a central (but quiet and calm) location, chic modern rooms, friendly staff, and a great breakfast. There is also a wonderful courtyard garden to escape to. The hotel's ethos is to provide the perfect romantic spot for couples. As such, it does not accommodate children under the age of 16, unless you are booking a suite. These are located in a separate building, just three minutes' walk from the main hotel. Each suite accommodates a maximum of four people.
ⓘ *10, plus 2 suites*
🚤 *Sant'Angelo* 🔄 🛗 🛜 🅾️
🅰️ *All major cards*

■ RESIDENCE CORTE GRIMANI

€€€

**CORTE 4402, CALLE GRIMANI
TEL 041 241 0719**

cortegrimani.com

This residence offers very stylish and centrally located apartments in a 17th-century palazzo—each apartment is named for a different Venetian artist. Clean, spacious, and equipped with washing machines, refrigerators, and safes, they make a perfect choice for families and groups. The reception staff are very helpful and this is a place you can really feel at home in Venice.

🚪 *15 apartments*
🚏 *Rialto* 🔄 🅿 📶 🔲
💳 *All major cards*

■ HOTEL FLORA

€€€

**SAN MARCO 2283A
TEL 041 520 5844**

hotelflora.it

In a secluded location at the end of a narrow alleyway, just off a bustling main street, the Flora is charming. It has a lovely tearoom, a gym offering shiatsu massage, and a garden that is positively irresistible in summer.

🚪 *40* 🚏 *Giglio* 🔲 📶 🔲 📺
💳 *All major cards*

CASTELLO

In convenient Castello, you are close to San Marco, and therefore the city's main attractions, but you are also a little way from the crowds. Major sights in Castello itself

include the **Scuola Grande di San Marco** (see pp. 78–79). Hotels along the waterfront at San Zaccaria make a good choice if you are looking for a view of the lagoon.

■ HOTEL LONDRA PALACE

€€€€€

**RIVA DEGLI SCHIAVONI 4171
TEL 041 520 0533**

londrapalace.com

This four-star palace overlooks the lagoon and several rooms have stunning views. The hotel is very tastefully decorated with Biedermeier furniture, lavish fabrics, and fine finishes. En suites have luxurious marble bathrooms. The staff are very helpful and it's definitely worth requesting a room with a balcony so that you can enjoy the view with a late-night glass of wine.

🚪 *53* 🚏 *San Zaccaria*
🔄 🔲 📶 🔲
💳 *All major cards*

■ AQUA PALACE

€€€€€

**CALLE DELLA MALVASIA 5492
TEL 041 296 0442**

aquapalace.it

This little gem of a hotel has spacious rooms decorated with a luxuriant style. Re-creating Venice of the 1500s, rooms feature antique wooden furniture and artifacts from the Far East. The standard breakfast includes cooked options as well as the normal continental fare. Staff are helpful and very knowledgeable.

🚪 *9, plus 6 suites and 9 junior suites*
🚏 *Rialto* 🔄 🔲 📶 🔲
💳 *Visa, MasterCard, American Express*

■ HOTEL SANT'ANTONIN

€€€€€

**FONDAMENTA FURLANI 3299
TEL 041 523 1621**

hotelsantantonin.com

This is a beautiful boutique hotel with subtle decor, and modern bathrooms. They serve up good breakfasts and there is a fantastic garden to relax in at any time of day. The hotel has two suites with private balconies: one overlooking the garden and the other overlooking the canal.

🚪 *13, including 2 junior suites*
🚏 *San Zaccaria*
🔄 🔲 📶 🔲
💳 *All major cards*

■ CA' DEI DOGI

€€€€

**CORTE SANTA SCOLASTICA 4242
TEL 041 241 3751**

cadeidogi.it

Located next to the Bridge of Sighs, this little palazzo offers a choice of six rooms and three different apartments. The position is great and the rooms are modern in style and sleek. Staff are extremely friendly and knowledgeable.

🚪 *6 rooms, plus 3 apartments*
🚏 *San Zaccaria* 🔲 📶 🔲
💳 *All major cards*

■ LIASSIDI PALACE

€€€€

**PONTE DEI GRECI 3405
TEL 041 520 5658**

liassidipalacehotel.com

A four-star boutique hotel housed in what used to be a Gothic palazzo. Located near the Ponte dei Greci, it is in an unusually quiet part of Castello, on one of the lesser-known canals. The neutrally decorated rooms are less extravagant than some other choices, but no less charming for it. The staff are friendly and the hotel is clean and comfortable.

(1) 26 🚤 *San Zaccaria*
🔁 🅢 🛜 🅢
🅢 *All major cards*

■ CASA NICOLÒ PRIULI
€€€
CASTELLO 4986
TEL 041 296 0639
casanicolopriuli.com
A quiet hotel on one of the lesser-known canals, very close to the Chiesa di San Zaccaria. All of the rooms are decorated with late 19th-century furnishings and fine velvets. Some rooms have views of the canal and private terraces. In summer, breakfast is served in a delightful leafy courtyard.

(1) 15 🚤 *San Zaccaria*
🔁 🅢 🛜 🅢
🅢 *Visa, MasterCard, American Express*

■ PALAZZO VITTURI
€€€
CAMPO SANTA MARIA FORMOSA 5246
TEL 041 241 0856
palazzovitturi.com
An overall impressive three-star hotel for a reasonable budget, this hotel has large rooms with typically Venetian high ceilings. Originally a Byzantine-Gothic palazzo

some of the rooms within have original stucco wall designs and beautiful ceilings. Book the Deluxe Double and you'll receive a complimentary breakfast in your room or on the nearby terrace.

(1) 16, *including 1 suite and 3 junior suites*
🚤 *San Zaccaria, Rialto*
🅢 🛜 🅢 🅢 *All major cards*

CANNAREGIO

Cannaregio is one of the best *sestieri* to stay in if you would prefer a quieter, off-the-beaten-track view of Venice. You are near the **Jewish Ghetto** (see pp. 102–103) here, and the lively strips of **Fondamenta della Misericordia** (see pp. 96–97) and Fondamenta degli Ormesini, both lined with funky bars and lively restaurants to keep you entertained at night. This neighborhood is also perfect for proximity to the train station and Piazzale Roma.

■ AL PONTE ANTICO
€€€€€
CALLE DELL'ASEO 5768
TEL 041 241 1944
alponteantico.com
A wonderful hotel, Al Ponte Antico is small and intimate. The seven rooms are opulent and spacious. Decorated in Louis XV style, the walls are covered in period-style wallpaper. Another highlight here is the hotel's Grand Canal Terrace, which overlooks the Rialto

neighborhood. Staying here will make you feel like a king.

(1) 7 🚤 *Rialto* 🅢 🛜 🅢
🅢 *Visa, Mastercard, American Express*

■ PALAZZO ABADESSA
€€€€
CALLE PRIULI 4011
TEL 041 241 3784
abadessa.com
This charming hotel was a former embassy. It has a perfect central location while offering the tranquillity of its own private courtyard garden. The garden is stunning and a beautiful place to relax with a prosecco. The rooms are very elegant, each fitted out in typical period style, complete with Murano chandeliers, antique furniture, and paintings.

(1) 15 🚤 *Ca' d'Oro* 🅢 🛜 🅢
🅢 *Visa, MasterCard, American Express*

■ HOTEL ANTICO DOGE
€€€
CANNAREGIO 5643
TEL 041 241 1570
anticodoge.com
A lovely hotel that captures the Venetian charm of some of the more expensive luxurious hotels, but at a very reasonable price. The rooms vary in size and are decorated in a classic Venetian style. Although the hotel is in a fantastic location, facing Campo dei Santi Apostoli, you can expect some noise come nighttime.

(1) 20 🚤 *Ca' d'Oro, Rialto*
🔁 🅢 🛜 🅢
🅢 *All major cards*

HOTELS

■ HOTEL ARCADIA
€€€
RIO TERÀ S. LEONARDO 1333
TEL 041 717 355
hotelarcadia.net
In this lovely boutique hotel, all the rooms are tastefully decorated with Venetian-style fabrics and wallpapers giving them a classic look while still being modern and sleek. The rooms are a good size and if you are arriving or leaving by train, access to the station is very straightforward. One thing to bear in mind is that the hotel could be noisy at night and early in the morning, as it is on a busy street.
ⓘ 17 ≜ San Marcuola-Casinò
🖨 🛜 ⓢ
🏧 All major cards

■ VILLA ROSA
€€€
CALLE DE LA MISERICORDIA 389
TEL 041 716 569
villarosahotel.com
A fabulous budget hotel close to Piazzale Roma and Calatrava's ultramodern Ponte della Costituzione (see p. 96). The rooms are comfortable—some of them furnished in period Venetian style—and the staff are very helpful.
ⓘ 33 ≜ Ferrovia 🛜 ⓢ
🏧 All major cards

SAN POLO

San Polo is one of Venice's oldest *sestieri*, and is at the heart of the city geographically. A hotel in this neighborhood is perfect for visiting the city's major sights, including the **Mercato di Rialto** (see pp. 114–115), the **Scuola Grande di San Rocco** (see pp. 122–125), and the **Basilica di Santa Maria Gloriosa dei Frari** (see pp. 120–121). There are a good number of shops to explore and many restaurants, and a vibrant nightlife. This area is ideal for the first-time visitor to the city and for the more budget-conscious traveler.

■ AMAN VENICE
€€€€€
CALLE TIEPOLO 1364
TEL 041 270 7333
aman.com
At the top of the scale for luxury and elegance, this hotel is famous for being George Clooney's choice on his wedding night. A relative newcomer to the hotel scene—it opened in 2013—the former 16th-century palazzo has 24 rooms (each decorated in its own unique style), opulent signature suites, two private gardens, and private boats. Its stunning facade on the Grand Canal was once painted by Paolo Veronese.
ⓘ 24 ≜ San Silvestro
🖨 🛜 ⓢ 📺
🏧 Visa, MasterCard, American Express

■ HOTEL L'OROLOGIO VENEZIA
€€€€
RIVA DE L'OGIO 1777
TEL 041 272 5800
hotelorologiovenezia.com
Highly recommended by all who stay here, this hotel is housed in a palazzo overlooking the Grand Canal, just five minutes' walk from the Ponte di Rialto. Fine watchmaking is the theme here, and many decorative items and ornaments reflect this. The decor is modern, spacious, and sleek, and staff are helpful and friendly. Rooms have been soundproofed, so you can expect peace and quiet. There is also a beautiful terrace snack bar where guests can relax and soak up the city.
ⓘ 43, plus 2 apartments and 6 rooms in a nearby building
≜ Rialto Mercato 🖨 🛜 ⓢ
🏧 All major cards

■ ANTICA LOCANDA STURION
€€€
CALLE DEL STURION 679
TEL 041 523 6243
locandasturion.com
If you look at Gentile Bellini's 15th-century painting of this area—"Miracle of the Cross at the Bridge of San Lorenzo," you'll see that this hotel was already in business. The three-star Sturion is one of the oldest inns still operating in the city. Situated on the top floor of a canalside palazzo, its beautifully furnished rooms have fantastic views of the Ponte di Rialto.
ⓘ 11 ≜ San Silvestro
🖨 🛜 ⓢ
🏧 All major cards

■ PENSIONE GUERRATO
€€€
CALLE DRIO LA SCIMIA 240/A
TEL 041 528 5927
hotelguerrato.com

TRAVEL ESSENTIALS

If you are looking for an area of the city with a lively, local nightlife, this is the spot for you, right beside the Ponte di Rialto. There are several late-night bars in the area, so things can get noisy after dark—not a problem if you are joining the crowd. Modern and comfortable, this is a good budget-friendly option.

🅘 20, plus 3 apartments
🅿 Rialto Mercato 🄪 🄢
🅢 Visa, MasterCard (reservation and payment), American Express

■ RIALTO 1082 B&B
€€–€€€
SAN POLO 1082
TEL 041 241 0164
rialto1082.com

This is an excellent little B&B in the heart of the Rialto area, conveniently situated beside the San Silvestro vaporetto stop. Staying here is a very personal experience. The owner is warm and welcoming, the soundproofed rooms are clean and comfortable, and the breakfasts are legendary. Excellent price for the location.

🅘 3 🅿 San Silvestro 🄪 🄲 🄢
🅢 Visa, MasterCard, American Express

SANTA CROCE

Close to Piazzale Roma, Santa Croce is perfect for anyone arriving by bus or car. Transfers to your hotel will be very straightforward. A number of accommodations in this sestiere offer Grand Canal views, yet

without the hustle and bustle of the city's main thoroughfares. There are also many hotels in quiet backstreets, for those wanting to experience the less tourism driven side of Venice. This neighborhood is ideal for visiting a number of significant churches and museums, namely **Ca' Pesaro** (International Museum of Modern Art; see pp. 116–117), **Palazzo Mocenigo** (see p. 117), and the **Fondaco dei Turchi** (Natural History Museum; see p. 49).

■ CA' NIGRA LAGOON RESORT
€€€€
SANTA CROCE 927, CALLE DE L'OGIO
TEL 041 275 0047
hotelcanigra.com

A splendid, small boutique hotel with a number of large period-style rooms and suites. The hotel is positioned in a lovely quiet spot, but is easily accessed from the train station or by boat. A former palazzo, the building is decorated in 18th-century style, complete with lavish furnishings, antique furniture, and many original architectural features. Some of the rooms overlook one of the prettiest canalside gardens in Venice.

🅘 22 🅿 Celestia 🄪 🄲 🄢
🅢 All major cards

■ SAN CASSIANO
€€€€
CALLE DEL ROSA 2232
TEL 041 524 1768
sancassiano.it

Once the home of Giacomo Favretto, one of the greatest

Venetian painters of the 19th century, this gem of a hotel is located on the Grand Canal. It's an exquisite, little red palace not far from the Mercato di Rialto. The public rooms and the first-floor balcony facing the canal make you feel like a visiting ambassador. The 36 rooms are beautifully furnished in true Venetian style, with rich hues of red and gold. They are small but perfectly adequate and the service is first rate.

🅘 36, plus 6 suites
🅿 San Stae 🄪 🄲 🄢
🅢 All major cards

■ HOTEL AL SOLE
€€€
SANTA CROCE 134–136
TEL 041 244 0328
alsolehotels.com

This lovely hotel is based in the wonderful 16th-century Ca' Marcello. It has a beautiful facade, foyer, and garden and is positioned on one of Venice's more charming stretches of canal. The rooms are completely modernized, but they do have a few period touches. The location is very convenient for Piazzale Roma and Campo Santa Margherita.

🅘 51 🅿 Piazzale Roma
🄪 🄲 🄢
🅢 All major cards

■ HOTEL PALAZZO GIOVANELLI
€€€
CAMPO SAN STAE 2070
TEL 041 525 6040
hotelpalazzogiovanelli.com

This opulent small hotel overlooks the Grand Canal on one side and the Chiesa di

San Stae on the other side; Ca' Pesaro is around the corner. You are close to all of Venice's major sights, yet from the peaceful courtyard garden at the entrance to the elegant rooms, the only sounds you will hear in this modernized palazzo are the tolling of the church bell and the boats passing beneath your window. A waterside door lets you arrive in a private taxi or gondola.

(1) *41* 🛶 *San Stae* ⬍
🟦 🛰 🟦 🟦 *All major cards*

DORSODURO

If you are interested in art, Dorsodoro is the place to stay. You will find the **Collezione Peggy Guggenheim** (see p. 135) and **Gallerie dell'Accademia** (see pp. 140–143) in this *sestiere,* alongside many little art galleries dotted along the winding streets of the district. **Campo Santa Margherita** (see p. 139) is nearby—a hub of Venetian nightlife with bars staying open until the early hours.

■ CENTURION PALACE
€€€€€
DORSODURO 173
TEL 041 34281
centurionpalacevenezia.com
This hotel gives the impression of old-style Venice with its Gothic facade, but once you step inside you encounter a futuristic twist. The decor is modern and contemporary with bold, bright colors and modernist furniture—a complete contrast to the old city around you. This is a great location for art lovers. There are many galleries in the area and the Collezione Peggy Guggenheim is only a short stroll away. You will find a mix of room sizes here. Some have little terraces while others have views of the canal, so check the website for the room you want before you book.

(1) *50, including 4 suites and 8 junior suites*
🛶 *Salute* ⬍ 🟦 🛰 🟦 🍸
🟦 *All major cards*

■ PALAZZO STERN
€€€€€
DORSODURO 2792/A
TEL 041 2770869
palazzostern.it
This is a charming hotel with great views over the Grand Canal. The 14th-century building has been beautifully restored, retaining all the old features but with the utmost attention to modern needs. Perhaps the best feature is the terrace overlooking the Grand Canal, a lovely place to have breakfast and watch the city wake up before your eyes. After a long day of sightseeing, you can wind down with a prosecco in the outdoor rooftop jacuzzi.

(1) *24, including 1 suite and 6 junior suites* 🛶 *Ca' Rezzonico*
⬍ 🟦 🛰 🟦 🟦
🟦 *All major cards*

■ CA' PISANI
€€€€
RIO TERRÀ FOSCARINI 979A
TEL 041 240 1411
capisanihotel.it
This is a great hotel in a lovely, quiet location, close to the Gallerie dell'Accademia. The first "designer hotel" in the city, its rooms have all the modern technology of the 21st century while reflecting a strong art deco influence with original furniture from the 1930s and 1940s. Two rooms cater specifically for the disabled and the hotel has it own bar and restaurant. Guests also benefit from a steam room.

(1) *29, including 6 suites*
🛶 *Accademia, Zattere*
⬍ 🟦 🛰 🟦 🟦 *All major cards*

■ HOTEL PAUSANIA
€€€
DORSODURO 2824
TEL 041 522 2083
hotelpausania.it
The Pausania was once a private palace on a tranquil side canal. Its entrance retains the original marble wellhead and exterior staircase, while the facade retains an original Gothic window. For a spot just between lively Campo Santa Margherita and Campo San Barnaba, this really is a surprisingly secluded option.

(1) *24* 🛶 *Ca' Rezzonico*
🟦 🛰 🟦 🟦 *Visa, MasterCard, American Express*

THE ISLANDS

A short hop by ferry from the main city, the Venetian islands of Giudecca, Murano, Torcello, and Lido offer a range of experiences. On the whole, they tend to be less crowded than Venice itself. At the budget end of the scale, try

Giudecca; for ultimate luxury, head to Lido. The latter is also the ideal beach destination in summer months. Some island hotels close for winter.

■ PALLADIO HOTEL & SPA
€€€€€
FONDAMENTA DELLE ZITELLE, GIUDECCA
TEL 041 520 7022
palladiohotelspa.com
Housed in two adjacent buildings on the island of Giudecca, this hotel is part of the prestigious Bauer complex that also has accommodations in San Marco (see p. 179). This was the first hotel in Venice to install a spa, and it makes for luxury living at its finest. The main building is a converted 16th century convent. Each of the 58 rooms are spacious and beautifully decorated. Many rooms have a lagoon view or overlook the hotel's stunning gardens, some have balconies.
🛈 58, plus 21 suites 🚤 Zitelle
🔁 🛗 🛜 🚭 🛗
🏧 All major cards

■ HOTEL EXCELSIOR
€€€€€
LUNGOMARE MARCONI 41, LIDO
TEL 041 526 0201
hotelexcelsiorvenezia.com
At the turn of the 20th century, the Excelsior was among the first European hotels to make a month at the seaside a fashionable vacation alternative. It is still huge, glamorous, and offers virtually everything you could want. In early September, it becomes base camp for the hordes of press and movie stars who flock here for the film festival.
🛈 197 🚤 Lido 🔁
🛗 🛜 🚭 ⛵ 🏧 All major cards

■ LOCANDA CIPRIANI
€€€
PIAZZA SANTA FOSCA 29, TORCELLO
TEL 041 730 150
locandacipriani.com
Rustic yet elegant, it has welcomed virtually every famous visitor to Venice in the past hundred years, from Hemingway to Queen Elizabeth II and dozens of Hollywood stars. The rooms are not large but are perfectly appointed, and in the winter a fire blazes in the foyer. Torcello's air of magical, remote tranquillity is perfectly mirrored by this small, peaceful hotel.
🛈 5 🚤 Torcello 🛗 🛗
🏧 Visa, MasterCard, American Express

■ MURANO PALACE
€€€
FONDAMENTA DEI VETRAI 77, MURANO
TEL 041 739 655
muranopalace.com
Overlooking the Rio dei Vetrai (Glassmakers' Canal), the Murano Palace could not have a more apt location. This charming boutique hotel has six rooms, four of them with a canal view. Each is decorated with precious Venetian fabrics and sparkling jewel-like chandeliers made by the hotel owners themselves.
🛈 6 🚤 Murano Colonna
🛗 🛜 🛗 All major cards

■ VILLA MABAPA
€€€
RIVIERA SAN NICOLÒ 16, LIDO
TEL 041 526 0590
villamabapa.com
Originally a private residence built in the late 1920s, the Villa Mabapa still retains a number of its original art nouveau features. The rooms are simply furnished in a contemporary style, some of them with views overlooking the hotel's beautifully landscaped gardens. Run by four generations of the same family, this hotel complex also includes the Villa Morea and Casa Pradel, located within the same grounds. The hotel has a restaurant serving Venetian cuisine, with tables in the garden in summer.
🛈 60 🚤 Santa Maria Elisabetta
🔁 🛗 🛜 🛗
🏧 All major cards

■ AL REDENTORE DI VENEZIA
€€–€€€
FONDAMENTA PONTE LUNGO 234/A, GIUDECCA
TEL 041 522 9402
alredentoredivenezia.com
This hotel has elegant apartments within easy walking distance of Giudecca's major sights, including the Punta della Dogana museum of modern art and the Basilica di Santa Maria della Salute. Contemporary in style, and with Venetian designer furniture, some rooms have exposed beams and parquet flooring. All of them have travertine bathrooms.
🛈 8 🚤 Salute 🔁 🛗 🛜 🛗
🏧 All major cards

LANGUAGE GUIDE

Useful Words & Phrases

Yes *Sì*; No *No*
Excuse me (in a crowd or asking for permission) *Permesso*; (asking for attention) *Mi scusi*
Hello (before lunch) *Buon giorno*; (after lunch) *Buona sera*
Hi or bye *Ciao*
Please *Per favore*
Thank you *Grazie*
You're welcome *Prego*
OK *Va bene*
Good-bye *Arrivederci*
Good night *Buona notte*
here *qui*
there *lì*
today *oggi*
yesterday *ieri*
tomorrow *domani*
now *adesso/ora*
later *più tardi/dopo*
this morning *stamattina*
this afternoon *questo pomeriggio*
this evening *stasera*
open *aperto*
closed *chiuso*
Do you have? *Avrebbe?*
Do you speak English? *Parla inglese?*
I'm American *Sono americano* (man); *Sono americana* (woman)
I don't understand *Non capisco*
Where is. . .? *Dov' è. . .?*
I don't know *Non so*
No problem *Niente*
My name is. . . *Mi chiamo. . .*
Let's go *Andiamo*
At what time? *A che ora?*
When? *Quando?*
What times is it? *Che ora è?*
I'd like. . . *Vorrei. . .*
How much is it? *Quanto costa?*

breakfast *la (prima) colazione*
lunch *il pranzo*
dinner *la cena*
appetizer *l'antipasto*
first course *il primo*
main course *il secondo*
vegetable, side dish *il contorno*
dessert *il dessert/dolci*
wine list *la lista dei vini*
I'd like to order *Vorrei ordinare*

Antipasto

sarde in saor fried sardines with sweet-sour onions
caparossoli local small clams steamed with garlic
seppioline small local cuttlefish
peoci mussels
baccalà mantecato creamy spread of dried cod

Pasta Sauces

all'amatriciana tomato sauce with chili and bacon
bigoli in salsa mild anchovy and onion
alla busera shrimp and tomato
alle vongole white clam sauce
al ragù bolognese sauce
col nero di seppia cuttlefish ink

Meats

fegato all veneziana liver and onions
la bistecca beefsteak
ben cotta well done
non troppo cotta medium
appena cotta rare
il filetto fillet steak
il carpaccio finely sliced raw beef
il maiale pork
il manzo beef
il pollo chicken
le polpette meatballs
il vitello veal

Fish & Seafood

le alici/acciughe anchovies
l'aragosta/astice lobster
il calamaro squid
i gamberetti shrimp
il granchio crab
il polipo octopus
le sarde sardines
la sogliola sole
il tonno tuna
il branzino sea bass
l'orata gilt-headed bream
il cefalo gray mullet
le seppie cuttlefish
grigliata mista mixed grilled fish
fritto misto mixed fried fish

Vegetables

l'aglio garlic
gli asparagi asparagus
il carciofo artichoke
la carota carrot
il cavolfiore cauliflower
i fagiolini fresh green beans
l'insalata mista/verde mixed/green salad
la melanzana eggplant
la patata potato
i piselli peas
i pomodori tomatoes
gli spinaci spinach
il tartufo truffle
le zucchine zucchini

Fruit

l'albicocca apricot
l'arancia orange
le ciliegie cherries
le fragole strawberry
la mela apple
la pera pear
la pesca peach
la pescanoce nectarine
il pompelmo grapefruit
l'uva grapes

INDEX

INDEX

INDEX

CREDITS

Authors

Joe Yogerst and Gillian Price

Additional text by: Helen Douglas-Cooper, Lisa Gerard-Sharp, Reg G. Grant, and Clare O'Connor

Picture Credits

t = top; b = bottom; l = left; r = right; m = middle

2–3 Ben Southgate. 4 Matteo Carassle/SIME/4Corners. 5tr Vadim Petrakokov/Shutterstock. 5mr Delpixel/Shutterstock. 5bl Treasury of San Marco, Venice, Italy/Bridgeman Images. 6 Olimpio Fantuz/SIME/4Corners. 9 Matthias Scholz/Alamy. 12–13 Luca Da Ros/SIME/4Corners. 14tm Ian Armitage. 14bl Peter Fosberg/Alamy. 15 Cameraphoto Arte Venezia/Bridgeman Images. 17 Yulia Grioryeva/Shutterstock. 18 mikecphoto/Shutterstock. 19tr Vladimir Daragan/Shutterstock. 19br Ian Armitage. 21 JOHN KELLERMAN/Alamy. 22 Piere Bonbon/Alamy. 23tr LOOK Die Bildagentur der Fotografen GmbH/Alamy. 23bl The Art Archive/Alamy. 24 © Peggy Guggenheim Collection, Venice. Ph. David Head. 26tl Musica a Palazzo. 26bl Bellini Cocktail, Bar Longhi, The Gritti Palace, a Luxury Collection Hotel. 27 anastasia buinovska/Shutterstock. 29 Ian Armitage. 30tl Geoffrey Taunton/Alamy. 30tr Matthias Scholz/Alamy. 30bl Etabeta/Alamy. 31tl hwo/imageBROKER/Superstock. 31tr Picavet/Getty Images. 31mr Karl F. Schöfmann/imageBROKER/Superstock. 31br Shutterstock. 32 National Museum Wales/Bridgeman Images. 34 gab90/Shutterstock. 35tr jozef sedmak/Alamy. 35br age fotostock/Alamy. 36 Johanna Huber/SIME/4Corners. 38tm Arcangelo Piai/SIME/4Corners. 38bl Piere Bonbon/Alamy. 39tr Olena Kachmar/123rf.com. 39br Arcangelo Piai/SIME/4Corners. 41 REDA &CO srl/Alamy. 42 David Angel/Alamy. 43tr Mauro Vianello/glasshandmade.com. 43br Marco Secchi/Getty Images. 44 LOOK Die Bildagentur der Fotografen GmbH/Alamy. 46 VizioVirtù Cioccolateria (www.viziovirtu

.com). 47tm Matthias Scholz/Alamy. 47br Jan Wlodarczyk/Alamy. 49 robert harding/Superstock. 50–51 Günter Gräfenhain/4Corners. 54 Maurizio Rellini/SIME/4Corners. 56 Marc Funda. 57 De Agostini Picture Library/G. Dagli Orti/Bridgeman Images. 58 Yamagiwa/Shutterstock. 61 lazyllama/Shutterstock. 63 Photograph by Delfino Disto Legnani and Marco Cappelletti. Courtesy of OMA. 64 Marc Funda. 66 Guido Cozzi/SIME/4Corners. 68 Treasury of San Marco, Venice, Italy/Bridgeman Images. 69 Pushkin Museum, Moscow, Russia/Bridgeman Images. 70 Villa Barbarigo, Noventa Vicentina, Italy/Bridgeman Images. 71 Johanna Huber/SIME/4Corners. 73 Jorge Royan/Alamy. 74 Radu Razvan/Shutterstock. 76tl Photoservice Electa/Universal Images Group/Superstock. 76bl Rolf E. Staerk/Shutterstock. 77tl Ian Armitage. 77tr Vadim Petrakov/Shutterstock. 78 Cristiano Fronteddu/Alamy. 81 Photoservice Electa/Universal Images Group/Superstock. 83 Lucian Milasan/Shutterstock. 84 National Geographic Creative/Alamy. 86 Pictures from History/Bridgeman Images. 87 Museo Correr, Venice, Italy/Bridgeman Images. 89 Jan S./Shutterstock. 91 LYSVIK PHOTOS/Shutterstock. 92 Rolf E. Staerk/Shutterstock. 94 Petr Jilek/Shutterstock. 95 RnDmS/Shutterstock. 97 Matthias Scholz/Alamy. 99 Ben Southgate. 100 T.C. Bird. 101 Renata Sedmakova/Shutterstock. 102 Marco Secchi/Getty Images. 104 © Sarah Quill/Bridgeman Images. 105 Royal Collection Trust © Her Majesty Queen Elizabeth II, 2016/Bridgeman Images. 107 Marco Secchi/Getty Images. 108 Arcangelo Piai/SIME/4Corners. 110 Hemis/Alamy. 112tl Guido Baviera/SIME/4Corners. 112bl Ian Armitage. 113 Imagno/Getty Images. 115 Arcangelo Piai/SIME/4Corners. 119 JOHN KELLERMANN/Alamy. 120 age fotostock/Alamy. 122 imageBROKER/Alamy. 124 Mondadori Portfolio/Getty Images. 125 Mondadori Portfolio/Getty Images. 126 mountainpix/Shutterstock. 127 Matteo Carassale/SIME/4Corners. 129 Delpixel/Shutterstock. 130 Sabine Lubenow/Alamy. 132 Hemis/Alamy.

133ml Marco Secchi/Getty Images. 133tr Ben Southgate. 134 Marc Funda. 136 Matthias Scholz/Alamy. 139 Guido Baviera/SIME/4Corners. 140 Ian Armitage. 142–143 Galleria dell'Accademia, Venice, Italy/Bridgeman Images. 144 San Pantalon, Venice, Italy/Bridgeman Images. 145 Galleria dell'Accademia, Venice, Italy/Bridgeman Images. 146 Santa Maria Gloriosa dei Frari, Venice, Italy/Bridgeman Images. 147 Palazzo Ducale, Venice, Italy/Bridgeman Images. 149 Dave Zubraski/Alamy. 150 Ioan Florin Cnejevici/Shutterstock. 152 T.C. Bird. 153tr age fotostock/Superstock. 153br Eye Ubiquitous/Superstock. 155 Guido Baviera/SIME/4Corners. 156 age fotostock/Superstock. 159 De Agostini Picture Library/G. Dagli Orti/Bridgeman Images. 160 Iiko Iliev/Shutterstock. 162 Museo Nazionale de Bargello, Florence, Italy/Bridgeman Images. 163 Verrerie/Bridgeman Images. 164 De Agostini Picture Library/Bridgeman Images. 165 De Agostini Picture Library/Bridgeman Images. 167 Stock Connection/Superstock. 168 taniavolobueva/Shutterstock. 170–171 PHOTOMDP/Shutterstock.

Front Cover: Gondolas: Paul Biris/Getty Images; Mask: Igor Normann/Shutterstock.

Spine: Prawit Sirnwong/Shutterstock.

Back Cover: Fondamenta della Misericordia: Matthias Scholz/Alamy.

CREDITS

Since 1888, the National Geographic Society has funded more than 12,000 research, exploration, and preservation projects around the world. National Geographic Partners distributes a portion of the funds it receives from your purchase to National Geographic Society to support programs including the conservation of animals and their habitats.

National Geographic Partners
1145 17th Street NW
Washington, DC 20036-4688 USA

Become a member of National Geographic and activate your benefits today at natgeo.com/jointoday.

For information about special discounts for bulk purchases, please contact National Geographic Books Special Sales: specialsales@natgeo.com

For rights or permissions inquiries, please contact National Geographic Books Subsidiary Rights: bookrights@natgeo.com

The information in this book has been carefully checked and to the best of our knowledge is accurate. However, details are subject to change, and the National Geographic publisher cannot be responsible for such changes, or for errors or omissions. Assessments of sites, hotels, and restaurants are based on the author's subjective opinions, which do not necessarily reflect the publisher's opinion.

Created by Toucan Books Ltd
Ellen Dupont, *Editorial Director*
Anna Southgate, *Editor*
Dave Jones, *Designer*
Autumn Green, *Editorial Support*
Merritt Cartographic, *Maps*
Marion Dent, *Proofreader*
Marie Lorimer, *Indexer*

ISBN: 978-1-4262-1776-0

Printed in Hong Kong

16/THK/1